Also by Susan Powter

Stop the Insanity!

The Pocket Powter

Food

C'mon America, Let's Eat!

Hey, Mom! I'm Hungry!

Sober...
and Staying That Way

The Missing Link in
the Cure for Alcoholism

Susan Powter

Simon & Schuster

SIMON & SCHUSTER
Rockefeller Center
1230 Avenue of the Americas
New York, NY 10020

Designed by Levavi & Levavi

Manufactured in the United States of America

10 9 8 7 6 5 4 3 2 1

Library of Congress Cataloging-in-Publication Data is available.

ISBN 0-684-81595-8

This publication contains the opinions and ideas of its author. It is intended to provide helpful and informative material on alcoholism and related matters. It is sold with the understanding that the author and publisher are not engaged in rendering medical, psychological counseling, or other professional services in the book.

The author and publisher specifically disclaim all responsibility for any liability, loss, or risk, personal or otherwise, which is incurred as a consequence, directly or indirectly, of the use and application of any of the contents of this book.

I wish she'd known that it wasn't her fault.

What was she really like?

How much of the disease became her and how much of it all was just who she was?

How on earth did she hang on one day at a time in such physical sickness?

What if she was treated for her disease?

Why didn't all the doctors, counselors, current recovery specialists tell her the truth?

I wonder who she really was.

I wish I'd known her.

I wanted to be a part of her.

I needed to love her and I wanted desperately for her to love me. . . .

This book was written so that these questions never have to be asked again. So the pain and the longing can end. So that movement forward can begin. So the truth can be told. So that the cycles can be broken.

Contents

!'''!

Introduction

Dear Boys:

Mama is sick. Really sick. I have a disease that is interfering with my life. Last night before I came home, I stopped off at the store to pick up your Valentine's gifts. Just before I did, I went to the liquor store and bought a bottle of scotch, which I sat in the parking lot and drank while I finished some phone calls and organized some paperwork.

After putting together your Valentine's baskets, I drove home, drinking almost three quarters of the bottle while I was driving.

By the time I got to the house, I was drunk. When I walked in the door I opened a beer and began to organize the catering, the flowers, the DJ, and everything else that needed to be finished before the first guests arrived for Rusty's birthday party. . . .

That was the letter I wrote to my children when I was ready to tell the truth about my drinking. It was the letter I carried around with me for my first year of sobriety.

It kept me grounded. It kept me honest.

My name is Susan Powter and I'm an alcoholic. Can you believe it? I couldn't for a long time. You see, I was one of the few leaves on the family tree that was convinced I wasn't going down with this damn thing, the disease of alcoholism. There isn't a branch on the old Powter tree that isn't loaded (pardon that one) with it.

From as far back as anyone has traced, there have been alcoholics and criminals (Australian—thank you very much, England) in the family. Grandfathers, great-granddads, brothers, sisters, uncles, moms, and me!

Oh, the "experts" argue and argue about whether it's genetic, not genetic, environmental, or inherited, but there isn't anyone who is alcoholic reading this, or anyone who grew up in an alcoholic home, that doesn't know, by doing the slightest investigation—not even having to go where Sherlock had to go—how simple it is to trace this disease as far back as you choose to look.

Nobody can tell me that alcoholism isn't in the genes. It doesn't make a bit of difference to me when the "experts" come to their conclusions (and when you see how little they understand, you'll agree), because I've seen it ravage my immediate family—heard about old Uncle So and So, who just couldn't manage after a couple too many, seen Aunty fall in her soup one too many times, lived with the mother, dealt with the brother, bailed them out, cleaned 'em up. But what really drives it home (nothing like feeling it when it's happening to you), I've lived it. I live with alcoholism.

I've had to come to terms with the understanding that something was controlling me. That's one of the hardest things I've ever said in my life.

I have no problem understanding how hard it is for a CEO of a multimillion-dollar company to stop long enough to say that he or she is being controlled by the bottle. I'm one of 'em.

It's sooo easy to understand how the mom who is busy "running and doing" can't admit that she is a drunk. I'm one of them.

There's no question that a responsible person has a little trouble admitting that they acted totally irresponsibly. I'm one of them.

Run a business, a family, have a good life, work toward a future with determination, strength, and focus, and I/you/we can't control whether we pick up the drink or not? Come on!

Ridiculous, but true.

It controls me. The bottle was running my life. A statement that needs to be felt and understood on such a core level before anything can change. Truth that is both terrifying and freeing at the same time. Certainly one of the most courageous things you'll ever say!

¡!!!

Every alcoholic stops drinking twelve thousand times. After every bad night it's always, *"That's it, no more, never again. I'm just gonna do it this time."* How many times have those words spilled out of our mouths? As many times as

"Please, God, if you could only stop the spinning, I'll . . ." And you/we mean it every time we say it.

Then it happens, again and again. No matter how bad it was the last time, you find yourself drunk again.

The last time I quit drinking before I quit drinking before I quit drinking, I called a friend, a very dear friend that I knew I could trust. I couldn't stop shaking, sweating, or vomiting. I was in a fetal position on a beautiful white-tiled bathroom floor of a $12,000-a-month Pacific Palisades home, my home.

I'd been there before (who hasn't been there on a really bad morning after?), but this time was different. Something had changed. Something inside felt different. I was scared, really scared, because I didn't understand how I, how anyone, could have had so much to drink the night before. How did it happen? Why did I let it happen? Why was I feeling so sick . . . saturated . . . poisoned?

I wanted help. And when help arrived, all I could say was, I'm sick. Rusty sat on the floor with me and listened. Listened to the shame, the terror, the truth.

Sure, I quit drinking that day. Who wouldn't after feeling that sick? I quit, my heart and soul filled with the conviction that I would never drink again. And then, six weeks later, "it happened." But this time it was worse.

!!

If you want to stop drinking and stay stopped, you have to do a whole lot more than just quit drinking.

How about getting treatment for your disease? The physical disease of alcoholism. The American Medical Association declared alcoholism a disease in 1957, thirty-nine years ago, and I'll ask you: what is the treatment for the disease of alcoholism?

You are about to find out what it is, why you haven't heard about it, and what you can do to make sure that your disease gets treated. And you will also become oh-so-familiar with the power of this thing. This monster that lives inside of you, the voice that over and over again has wiped out all rational thought in your brain and continues to slip in one clear-as-a-whistle, perfectly reasonable thought . . .

Hey, have a drink!
It's OK, it's just one.
The other night wasn't really that bad . . . Come on,
    everyone drinks. Have one . . .

You are going to learn to recognize its amazing ability to seduce, charm, convince, and work you like nothing's ever worked you before—*and* how to answer it back, develop another voice, your voice, the rational voice, truth, reason, and treatment!

!ʼ!ʼ!ʼ

How many times have you quit drinking? It's impossible to remember all the times that I was convinced that my life, my children, my job, all the things that were very important to me, would be reason enough to quit—to just stop and stay stopped. And then it would happen. It never failed. Days, weeks, sometimes months into not drinking, that moment hit. That moment—when I had *"just one after work," "just one 'cause it's been a hard day," "just one and only one."* That moment when you reach for the one and end up having five, eight, fifteen . . .

Not anymore. Not with this powerful, updated current recovery thinking that you have in your hand.

Once you understand that it doesn't "just happen" to any of us, the minute you understand how much work (an enormous amount of biochemical and emotional work) goes into drinking again.

If you want that moment back, that moment you make the wrong decision, to drink again, to be yours—rational, balanced, in your control, not powerless, but so very powerful you couldn't imagine—you can have it. You will have all the tools you need to turn that moment of decision into a moment that can change your life forever: a moment of sobriety.

I know now, without a shadow of a doubt, that there's no chance in hell that I'll ever be able to sit down and have just one glass of wine, one beer after work, or a cocktail just to take the edge off, and I know how not to.

I'm so completely and absolutely certain about the fact that this disease—and alcoholism is a progressive, fatal disease that does not discriminate: smart, dumb, educated, uneducated, every color in the rainbow, religion, upbringing, none of it makes much of a difference at all when you drink, if you are alcoholic—I am certain that this disease can be easily managed, for much longer than one day at a time. I know you/I can live our lives without shame and the fear that you will drink "again someday." You can handle what needs to be handled. Heal what needs to be healed. Addiction, the great equalizer, is not a moral dilemma. This thing that's got control over your life isn't a willpower problem. You have a disease, and there is a cure for that disease.

I am sooo very sure of all of this now that nothing could budge me. I wouldn't take a sip of alcohol if you had a gun to my head (having my head blown off would be an easier way to die than the way I was dying). No chance of it.

Sober and clean and thrilled to be there is where I'm at, but getting there . . . it didn't just happen, and it won't just happen for you.

Waiting for the right time to quit, the motivation? Well, there is none. There is always a reason to drink when you are addicted to alcohol. Over and over again you've proven to yourself that you can't quit just because you said you were going to last week or last night. What's gonna make it different this time? What's your plan? How are you going to stay stopped?

One day at a time, fine, but please, experts contend that AA has a 12 percent recovery rate. What happens to the other 88 percent of us?

There is sooo much more available today in the field of alcoholism recovery. Have you heard about the wonderful scientific studies done over the last decades in the field of the biochemistry and the connection to your sobriety?

How about the amazing sugar connection? Have you made it yet? Have you ever heard the term *rational recovery?*

When my drinking got "out of control," I started reading, reading. Everything I could get my hands on about the subject of alcoholism. And I started hearing things like . . .

The susceptibility of alcoholism centers in two areas of the body: the liver and the brain.

The great majority of alcoholics experience blood sugar problems.

An abnormal metabolism in the liver that produces large quantities of acetaldehyde. This is the foundation for a comprehensive theory that explains susceptibility to alcoholism.

This susceptibility exists before the alcoholic ever starts to drink.

Alcoholics have a built-in, inherent, uncontrollable reaction to alcohol that causes them to become addicted when they drink.

Alcoholics don't abuse alcohol; alcohol abuses them.

AA may have opened the closet, but just a crack. We need to open the door wide, let a whole lot of light in, and clear out all of the cobwebs.

Aren't you interested in the proven methods (98 percent recovery rates) that can help you stay sober without calling your sponsor every time you feel like a drink? Want to take away the urge to drink completely? Wouldn't it be great to have a daily battle plan to stay sober and feeling better than you have in years? Don't you deserve everything that's out there in the fast-growing, wonderful field of alcoholism recovery?

Just think about what an advantage it would be for you to understand the stages of your disease, to get the answers to the questions that we all have, to face the fears, the shame, to stop the hiding, to start the acknowledging, so that you can get on with the solution. Sobriety. It's got to be discussed, and it is right here—honestly, openly, based in facts and truth, reference after reference—for you when you need it.

The information you are about to read, the facts that will astound you, the plans that will be there for you are all a part of what's really going to make a difference this time. It doesn't matter how many times you've tried to quit before, this time you can stay stopped.

In this book you will get the answers that I and millions of us needed to get sober and stay sober.

Having trouble controlling your drinking? Seem to be losing control? Under a lot of pressure and drinking more alcohol? Whatever you want to call it, if you feel there is something wrong and want to know more about it . . . read on!

Recognizing Alcoholism

!''!

Are you alcoholic?

Or are you a problem drinker?

Just under a lot of stress and drinking a little more than usual?

Is it alcoholism—or just your mother-in-law—that's driving you to drink?

Recognizing alcoholism. What a subject! There are a few of ways you can do it if you're interested.

a. You could take one of those little quizzes in the back of your favorite monthly magazine.
b. You could ask your doctor (you want clueless? you can't imagine!). Or
c. You could talk to someone who knows someone who knows someone who actually is an alco-

holic, and compare symptoms. Or you can do this: get really, really honest about your drinking.

To recognize something means *to see it*. I'll ask you: YOU HAVEN'T SEEN THAT YOUR DRINKING IS A PROBLEM?

To recognize means *to become familiar with*.

Your drinking hasn't become all too familiar? The bad endings. The hangover. The decision over and over again that gets you the same end result—disaster!

You don't know that your drinking is different? Different from the person who actually has one glass of wine with their salad? You need a quiz to recognize that your drinking is different???

You already recognize something. Don't you?

Here's what you need more than an "Alcoholic—are you or aren't you?" test. You need an honest, safe environment, with no judgment or shame. Just the truth about our drinking and a quick discussion on *alcoholism*.

I'm not sure there is a more important step in sobriety than getting to the truth about your drinking, because once you/I/we get honest, have a look at what's really going on (otherwise known as the truth), we can begin to create space for a solution.

You want to know if you are really, really, really alcoholic? Like, *alcoholic!* That's a big word. Alcoholic! Not just a problem drinker? Not just under a lot of stress? Not just a party kind of guy/gal?

Alcoholic???

You've seen the commercials about the "problem drinkers."

The wife pacing back and forth waiting for the husband to come home, knowing full well that it's another night of . . .
   He walks in the door.
   Drunk.
   Angry.
   Belligerent.
Strong, sad voice says:
"If you can't get help with us, get it somewhere."
Scary music.
Fade-out.

How about the man at the bar with his buddies.
   Getting louder by the second.
   Ad ends with:
   "HEY, BARTENDER, GIVE ME ANOTHER ONE . . ."
   Ad fades.
   Scary music.
   Fade-out.
   (You know all his friends have gone home after their one or two "responsible" drinks . . .)

He finally staggers out.
   Drives home drunk, puts the world in danger because he's such an irresponsible jerk and just can't control himself.
   Boy, oh boy, thank God we aren't him!

You've had a few nights here and there of a tad too much to drink, sure. But that's totally different from the guy on the commercial, with the really obvious, acting-like-a-totally-irresponsible-fool drinking PROBLEM. We are different from that belligerent, loudmouthed guy. We don't act like him.

And just to add another complication to this complicated matter of figuring out if you even have a problem . . . what if you are a woman?

Don't see a commercial with a woman staggering in the door? Female alcoholics don't even have the advantage of seeing a commercial on tele. It isn't shown. Ever seen it? I've never seen the husband pacing back and forth worrying about the marriage with the wife 'cause she's stumbling in the door.

I'm confused. Women don't sit at the bar and say, "HEY, BARTENDER, GIVE ME ANOTHER ONE"? Apparently it's not just Hollywood that's low on roles and lower on the pay scale for women. Apparently the recovery field is short on roles for women also.

!¡!!

So let's get back to the bar. What if you've never sat at the bar and gotten obnoxious? Maybe it's at the business lunch you are getting your fix? Driving the school bus, hungover again? Taking the baby-sitter home after just a few too many? Are you one of the world's top athletes? My son's teacher?

Have you ever woken up one too many mornings so hungover you could die? Have you wondered for days about what you said or did the last time you sat down for "just a couple" of drinks to unwind? Have you noticed lately that the "couple" has turned into more than you could have ever imagined? Have you ever gotten that cold, horrifying feeling inside when you see the ads for help on TV? Then maybe you, like me, are living/dying with alcoholism.

You may be the only one, at this point, who knows something is wrong. But you know if it is. Your drinking may still be easy to sweep under the "socially acceptable" rug, even though you have that nagging feeling that you drink differently than most. It may only be bad once in a while, and not difficult to cover up when it is. OK, a problem—but *alcoholic?* Why say the word? Why bring it up? Why bother with sobriety when the problem is really not that bad?

Great question, and one that I've got the best answer for . . .

HELLO . . .

EXCUSE ME.

FITNESS EXPERT.

Admit to being alcoholic???

FIT AS A FIDDLE.

WON'T PUT LOW-QUALITY, HIGH-FAT FOOD IN MY BODY.

And drinking myself to death???

DOING TV.

WRITING BOOKS.

RAISING THE GREATEST KIDS ON THE PLANET (EXCEPT YOURS, OF COURSE).

DOING SEMINARS ALL OVER THE COUNTRY.

LOVING MY LIFE.

LOVING MY WORK.

LEAN, STRONG, AND HEALTHY AS HELL . . .

• • •

If anyone has a "Why would ya open this can of worms?" clause in their life, it's me!

Write a book about it and expose an addiction? I never would have if I'd . . . I had a choice.

There is no way on earth that I would have gone through the last two years of facing truths that I didn't want to face, being so vulnerable I felt like I was going to die, feeling such shame in the midst of the most "success" I've ever had in my life, if there had been a choice. Addiction isn't a choice. Alcoholism isn't a choice. It's a textbook spiral down. The same end result for all of us. Nobody understands "socially acceptable" drinking— being enormously productive *and* addicted—more than me. I was.

But I also know the importance of opening this can of worms. I know that you are soooooo tired of it. There isn't any question that you are hurting, physically and emotionally. You may not know it yet, but if you are alcoholic, you are physically dying, poisoning every cell in your body, and there's no question that the last couple of parties . . . late nights with one too many . . . have left you scared to death.

I know you've woken up at whatever time of the morning and felt the guilt, the shame, the burden, the fear, the anger. Why talk alcoholism?

So we can get on with the solutions, the healing, the answers we need to get rid of it.

Recognizing, acknowledging, getting truthful about what's going on with the bottle in your life is one of the most important things you can do.

One of my biggest problems in recognizing my disease was how unbelievably educated I am when it comes to this "drinking problem" thing.

Oh, my God, one of the most educated drinkers you've ever met about alcoholism . . . that's me.

Math? Count me out.

Geography? Forget about it. I couldn't tell you where Arkansas is. Then again, why would you want to know? (Only joking, everyone in Arkansas—so I had one bad experience there that I can't seem to let go of. Call me immature, revengeful, or just plain childish.)

I know basic physiology. Had to spend some time looking into that—260 pounds, obesity, losing 133 pounds, changing lifestyles. Learned that, did that.

But educated, as in well schooled, as in knowing the presidents of the U.S.—forget about it.

Count me out, unless it's alcoholism you are hankering to know alllll about. If so, it's me you should be calling.

I don't mean call me now that I'm sober. I mean you could have called me after a couple-too-many beers and I could have told you more about alcoholism than anyone you know! Give me one ringy-dingy when my disease was in full swing, progressing into the toilet beautifully, and I could have told you all about progression.

If it's denial you wanted to know about—got it. Could have talked for hours on denial.

Don't even hesitate if it's drinking patterns you are interested in. I knew all there was to know about the patterns of alcoholics.

Textbook lifestyle changes? Knew that. We could have chatted up a storm . . .

• • •

My schooling started early. Eleven years old and sitting at an Al-Anon meeting desperate for some answers about what was swallowing our family alive . . . alcoholism.

Educated??

Who goes to an Al-Anon meeting at eleven alone?

I'd say that was looking for answers . . .

Knowledgeable?

Who sat with the sponsors and asked questions? ME.

Who went through years and years of living with alcoholics (and OH what fun that is) and seeing what this horrific disease does to a person's logic, love, being—their life? It destroys. I've seen it more times than even I want to know about.

I'm with ya when it comes to doing it *one day at a time.*

Nobody understands *sponsorship,* and *surrendering to your higher power,* and *attending meetings* better than me.

I know *it's an art to listen.*

Easy does it? Second nature to me.

Ninety meetings in ninety days? Been there.

And the *Serenity Prayer?* Could recite that at the drop of a hat!

My God, I've seen what alcohol does to a person's life. The pain, the torture of this disease. Not just once, twice, but three times in my own family . . . and boy, oh boy, was I relieved years ago when I knew that I missed the "genetic whatever-it-is."

WOW. Three out of six in a family down . . .

Thank goodness I was one of the lucky ones who could sit down like a normal person and enjoy a beer once in a while.

Thank God there were great-volleyball-playing, cooler-full-of-beer, guys-with-rippled-abs fun times on the beach ahead for me!

One of the lucky ones. I missed it! Phew . . . wipe that brow and have a beer. And that's exactly what I did for years.

And I must say that, without the self-righteous tone of a less alcoholism-educated person, I did watch what was happening to the less lucky (the ones with the unlucky genes), the alcoholics around me, and thought . . .

Just stop, damn it!
What's the matter with you?
You have so much to lose.
Don't allow this in your life.
Take control.
Get a grip.
Reach out for help before it ends in disaster.
Or . . .
Lazy?
Lacking willpower?
Maybe just not caring enough . . . ?

That's what I was thinking, not self-righteously, but thinking it all the same.

¦∭¦

Recognizing alcoholism isn't easy because there is no characteristic of an alcoholic. We are everyone. Living everywhere. You don't need to end up in the gutter before you stop this thing from destroying your life. It is more than possible to stop the pain and suffering that goes on every time you drink. There's no question that you can be living your life (what appears to be a good one on the surface) and dying of alcoholism. Millions of us are. And there is no question that there is treatment for your disease.

Why tell the truth about your drinking? So you can get on with the solution and get on with your life.

Simple!

Interested?

Let's start with the butt-honest facts about alcohol, shall we . . . ?

Sober Why

!"!

Here's what we are going to do. You and I are going to get the *why* of sobriety before we get the *sober how,* and I'll tell ya why. Because we get the *why* of everything else, that's why. The way I saw it then (in the beginning of sobriety) and now (as a veteran) is that we know the *why*s surrounding most of the other major decisions we make in our lives.

You know why you are living where you are living, or why you aren't living where you want to be living!

Hopefully you know why you date / marry / have sex with the person or people (OH, you nasty girl) you date, marry, or have sex with.

I'll bet you can tell me more than I ever wanted to know about why you bought the car you did. It's practical . . . works for the family . . . the kids . . . the dogs.

Maybe you are one of those over-fifty guys who bought the car for their image . . . Of course, if you are, you prob-

ably can't tell me much about why you do anything, because there's a good chance you are lying to yourself and
everyone around you. But that's a whole other book.

Midlife males. Don't they know that young thaannng
in the passenger seat of their sports car isn't there because
of them?

A better question would be, *sober why not?*

God, giving up alcohol forever and not having a clue
why you should? Doesn't make any sense, because giving
up alcohol is a big deal. Just ask anyone.

Ask them if they would miss a glass of wine with dinner
(don't ask an alcoholic, because we don't have one glass
of anything) or a nice cold beer once in a while if they
knew that it would never happen again. No more drinking,
ever, in their lives? Miss it? Sure they would.

Anything that is this woven into our society (OY, when
you hear how completely and absolutely entrenched in our
thinking a drinky-poo is, the "Why you should know the
sober why in order to stop and stay stopped" is gonna make
a whole lot of sense) is gonna be missed.

And to us alcoholics? Come on!

Cut back, maybe. Deal with what's turned out to be
"quite a problem recently," fair enough. But give it up
forever??? That's one hell of a statement.

So we have to talk about *why* before we talk about *how*
because that's the way it works—sobriety, that is—just
like everything else in our life.

Let's find out what you want . . . why you may (or may
not) want it . . . And what you have to do to get it (that
would be *how*). And then you do the work necessary to

maintain it. That's how it usually happens with most things. Don't see why sobriety should be any different!

There are two big sober *why*s. The first is my (and thousands of other alcoholics') opinion about "the reaping after the sowing," "the harvest after the planting," the "What am I getting in return for not drinking?" reasons why. Wait till you make the magic, peace, freedom, power, and control connections to sobriety that you may never have made, or even thought about until now!!! Fabulous stuff, and good, good reasons for sobriety.

Then there are the other *why*s. The "boat-rocking" *why*s of sobriety.

> Why your disease makes you sooo socially unacceptable.
> Why the government wants you to keep drinking no matter what the price.
> What the "hospitality" industry has in store for you.
> Why you haven't been given the treatment for your disease.
> Why you would ever, ever, ever think you could get (and stay) sober given what's happening with the current recovery thinking.

So many *why*s and sooo many interesting answers!

I've got a little story for you. The story of my first meeting as an alcoholic with other alcoholics. The meeting was at my home. Rusty, my manager (so Hollywood, wouldn't you say?) organized a group of four or five women for me to meet with.

I had spent some time with one of the women at a restaurant a couple of days before the big meeting, Rusty, Ruth and I, talking about being addicted to alcohol—fun lunch! Not that Rusty and Ruth (sounds like a steak house) didn't do everything in their power to make me as comfortable as I could be. They did, but there was nothing in the world that could have taken the bottomless pit of shame and fear out of my stomach that day.

Rusty was at the table with Ruth when I arrived. Ruth couldn't have been (and couldn't be) a lovelier human being. But I knew that she knew, and I knew that her knowing was closer to having no way out. (That was not a misprint. It's exactly how I felt walking toward the table for my first confessional alcoholic lunch.)

I raced through lunch, half listening to Ruth talking about drinking, the pain, *one day at a time*. La, la, la, la . . . I made some urgent excuse to leave. Loved Rusty, thought Ruth was just wonderful, was really glad she was sober, never thought I would be—and couldn't wait to get the hell out of there.

It was during that lunch—don't remember at what point—that it was decided for me (wasn't exactly the captain of my own ship that day) that a meeting would be set up at my home with some other alcoholic women. Just a suggestion! A thought. Hey, why not? Sit around, have a chat with a bunch of alcoholic strangers. My idea of a fun afternoon. But apparently necessary and the first step in getting some help for what was "out of control" in my life.

A meeting at the house worked for me because it left me with one or two less things to worry about . . .

a. I didn't have to go to a church basement to meet with a bunch of alcoholic strangers.

b. The afternoon time slot was good because of the kids. My children were at school, so who was to know anything about it????

> Nobody would have a clue that this little meeting was about alcohol, addiction, or any other kind of a problem. Just a midday meeting of women.

Picture this. Five (fabulous) women, one well-known actress that I had grown up watching on tele, sitting in my den. As far as I knew at the time (sounds like I'm in a deposition, doesn't it?) no one there knew that it was the buzzed-cut fitness queen that was the drunk (could have been the agent—very discreet, this anonymous thing), and everyone was respectful or experienced enough not to ask, "Done this before?"

Thank you, thank you, thank you, to this day, to those wonderful women for acting like coming over to a stranger's house in the middle of the afternoon was a perfectly normal thing to do. Anyway, everyone sat down and started making small talk with Rusty for what turned out to be a very long, uncomfortable period of time because I wasn't in the den with them.

I was busy wiping the counters thin, polishing the dishes, refilling every snack tray the second someone took a bite of food. Closets were organized, more food was cooking on the stove (in case someone started to starve to death), the kitchen-herb seedlings were being placed in cheesecloth (germinating, you know) because I couldn't (I'm not talking *didn't want to,* that's *couldn't*) sit down.

My insides were aching with fear. I was too frightened to think. Too close to what I had been avoiding like the plague for years to even consider feeling anything. Of course it all fell into the category of

> *Once they know it's me, they'll . . . ???*
> *I'm on TV. What will they think?*
> *Oh God, what happens if someone goes to the tabloids
>   and says something? "Blah, blah, blah . . ."*
> *What's gonna happen when they know it's me with the
>   drinking problem???*

Like they didn't already? What, the manic cleaning wasn't giving it away? These experienced, sober used-to-be - drunks - like - yo u - never - who've - gone - through -this-process-helping-hundreds-of-other-alcoholics didn't see the neon sign flashing over my head?

SUSAN'S GOT THE DRINKING PROBLEM

AND

SHE'S JUST A LITTLE NERVOUS RIGHT NOW!

After it got ridiculous enough, everyone sitting around talking, sitting in my den, eating my food, except me, it came to me, the answer! Sheer brilliance. The only thing that got me in the chair.

*I don't have to say anything. This is anonymous. I could just be anonymous, or—*my shifty little brain thought—*I'll just say it's research for a* book. *Yeah, that's it. Research for . . .*

Women, Wellness, and Addiction.

Or a coffee-table book! Women Having a Chat in the Middle of the Afternoon, *by Susan Powter.*

Women and something, research about women and something! That's the ticket.

That's what got me from the sink (thought it would be a good time to Ajax the hell out of the enamel) to the doorway of the den and almost to the chair, because by the time I got three feet into my walk to the chair, it had all changed. I went from the sheer brilliance of deception and lying to anger—from the world's sneakiest researcher/alcoholic to pissed off.

All because these women were alcoholics didn't mean that everyone who was drinking a little too much was.

Then I got defensive. *There's no need to admit to anyone that this drinking thing has been a little difficult lately. You can control it, you just haven't put your mind to it. Dedicate the time and energy and you can beat it. You don't need to tell them anything.*

And then? Fear. I got frightened. *If I tell them I'm alcoholic, then I'm never gonna be able to say I'm not. Once you say it, then what?*

"Listen, about that alcoholic comment the other day. Don't know what came over me. Silly me, what was I thinking? Alcoholic? Just kidding. Temporary insanity? And you know what we have to do with the insanity . . ." (Come on, you can't blame me for that one!)

Anything and everything was going off in my brain to

distract me from what I was really feeling, which was scared to death. There was nothing in me that wanted to sit in that chair and tell these women that I was alcoholic, that I was more frightened than I'd ever been in my life, that I didn't know how to stop drinking, didn't believe I could, and needed help. I was scared to death, or close to what I'm sure it feels like.

I got to the chair just as someone was telling a few jokes. I don't remember what they were, but right after the joke (or perhaps because I'd finally sat down), someone else started talking about what alcohol had done to their lives.

"So many nights when I was too drunk to put my kids to bed."

(I'm thinking, *You . . . the PTA-looking mother of all time? I can't even picture you having a drink, let alone guzzling enough booze to be too blurry-eyed to put your kids to bed.*)

"I promised myself never again . . . and the next morning I found myself at the fridge reaching for a beer. It was only ten A.M."

(I'm dying here. This tiny little woman with the normal-looking hair having a brewsky at 10 A.M.?)

"I woke up with men I didn't know, feeling like I was going to die, over and over again . . ."

"I was carrying my baby and dropped her because I was drunk."

"The fights my husband and I had when we were drunk . . ."

(Like right from the Junior League meeting, or what???)

• • •

The women I was sitting with got drunk! Let's start there. And the stuff that was coming out of their mouths!

You don't get more "normal" looking than these women. Wow, wow, wow, wow . . . They told their stories and I couldn't get enough. Not the gore or the pain—I couldn't get enough of the way they were talking about some of the things I'd just lived through and never, ever thought I'd be able to live with. Forget about being able to share and smile at the end of saying it in front of a complete stranger!

I listened and listened, and after a while something else besides fear and shame crept in. I was captivated. Enthralled. There was something they all had that I wanted. Their stories were different, but they all had one thing in common that afternoon, and it had nothing to do with disease and destruction.

It had everything to do with healing and light. And sitting there with them, I wanted that more than I wanted a beer.

I saw it in their eyes every time they talked about sobriety. The spark that was there in each of them whenever they shared the regaining of their lives.

The excitement in their faces when they talked about not drinking ever again.

They lit up when they mentioned what had happened in their lives since sobriety was their reality. Their lives now that they were not drinking held appreciation, gratitude, and joy . . . for all of them!

And I was greedy for it. They had grace. They were at peace with and in sobriety.

None of them had any fear at all when it came to their

drinking, even though they were talking so honestly about the suffering I was running from. They were happy *and* they had a disease for the rest of their lives? They were at peace?

Sober and peaceful? Why—there's that *why*—why were they so happy, so content, so excited, and so sure and dedicated to staying that way? Come on, how did that happen? How did they go from what I was feeling—fear, shame, having no clue how it was all going to happen or if it ever could, what you are feeling reading this if you are alcoholic—to what they were feeling?

Wow, what a meeting! We finish it up, the ladies get ready to leave. Definitely a group-hug moment. I was much more involved than I had been when they first came. That wouldn't have taken much, other than being present.

I wasn't feeling quite as ashamed. I felt stronger and a little more confident about the possibility of sobriety, until I walked the last lady out to her car and walked back in my front door, back into my life.

The minute I got inside I heard a clear, seductive message. The voice that gently suggests every time:

Have a drink!

How about a beer?

It's been a really long, tiring, difficult day.

Anyone who hasn't tried to quit drinking over and over again (all the nonalcoholics out there) doesn't have a clue what we are talking about right now, but you do. You know the voice, the drinker's logic, the strong, completely clear (at the moment) message that this would be the PER-FECT time to have a drink!

• • •

All the confidence and conviction I'd felt moments before drove off with the last alcoholic woman.

Just like every other time I'd said I was gonna stop drinking, the instant chorus in my brain, the drinking chorus, was telling me why I should just have one and sit down and think about everything that was said about this sobriety thing!

Give it some time to sink in. Have a beer and rest.

It's interesting information. Have a beer and digest it.

I'll tell ya what. Have a beer, pick the boys up from school, and relax.

There's some sensible advice just after a meeting about alcoholism . . .

Here's what I thought about, standing at the fridge, thinking about reaching for—with my arm outstretched, hand almost on—the bottle neck at that moment.

I thought about getting fit. Sure, it's true. My brain traveled back to the first walk I took at 260 pounds.

Making the decision to drop 133 pounds and that moment at the fridge had more in common than you could ever imagine—and probably more than you could ever imagine any human being has the chutzpah to try and tie together at this very moment. You see, when I was overfat, unfit looking, and feeling horrible, and made the decision to get well and get my life back, the first step, literally, was going for a walk.

I had the fitness level of a slug. So the walk was slow, slow, slow. I had no cardio-endurance to speak of. Walking up two stairs (that's not two flights, that's two stairs) was a triathlon for me at the time. I had very little muscular strength. (I mean, it's not as if I'd been pumping iron on a regular basis. I was schlepping around 43 percent of my total body weight as fat.) We're not talking speed walker when I say I went for that first walk.

Fitness wasn't my life thirty minutes later? I didn't find God on that walk? My commitment and motivation wasn't cemented during those thirty short minutes?

There was no instant cure for being incredibly unfit and overfat, but "something" did happen on that walk, and it was the same something that was happening years later at the fridge.

On that walk I'd had a glimpse . . . a moment of possibility, a look at something I'd been totally disconnected from for years.

When I got home from that walk (still 260 lbs.—that doesn't change in thirty minutes), I did have a little bit of energy. I started to make some connections.

Maybe, just maybe, I could feel that energy more often in my life?

If movement burns fat, maybe I could burn a ton of it and be lean someday?

I even went as far as thinking, hoping, that the muscles that felt like they were waking from the dead could, someday, maybe, feel that way all the time.

Get out. How mad could I go? (Remember, I was living in Garland, Texas, so the truly amazing thing was that sanity had been sustained at all . . . You'd think I could get past it all these years later, wouldn't ya?)

After my walk I felt better. Not perfect, just better. I got a tangible example of what was . . . maybe . . . sort of . . . if I could ever, ever do it . . . possible???

Hope. The possibility of? The chance to feel well and

healthy? See the connection? Years later, sober? The possibility of? The chance to have it someday? Who knew *Sober How* that day, standing at that fridge, but *maybe???*

I didn't have the answers yet.

Had no clue how it was gonna happen.

Didn't feel like I could enter the New York Marathon of Sobriety, but . . .

The magic of real possibility is what I'd gotten from the wonderful women who'd come to speak with me that afternoon. That's what I felt. That's what stopped me from drinking that afternoon. I got the glimpse of a really good reason why I should take my hand off the neck of the bottle and not drink that day. Something other than *Gotta stop drinking because there is something wrong with me,* something other than blame and shame. Something real. Magic and peace.

One really good *sober why* reason. MAGIC and PEACE.

¡!!!

What do you think? Lovely, but just a little on the spacey side for you? A tad New Agey? Not tangible enough? Need something that you could write home about, and magic and peace just ain't gonna cut it?

All right, not to worry. There's much more to *sober why* than just peace and magic. (Listen to that statement if you want to know how ass-backwards things in our world are. Need something bigger than peace and magic? What more is there?) And the other *whys* are much more concrete, and certainly concepts that we are more familiar

with . . . how about FREEDOM, POWER, and CON-
TROL? There's something we can grab hold of, as soon as
we put the drumstick and club down!

Freedom

The cornerstone of our country!

From the land of the FREE to the home of the brave
. . . it's freedom, baby!

You are an adult. You live in America and you are . . .
free.

Free to do whatever you want to do. And when it comes
to drinking, you bet you are free to do it. Drink up, because
nobody can tell you what to do, it's your life. Whose business is it that you like to drink once in a while? No one's!
You are over twenty-one. (Yeah, like anyone waits till they
are twenty-one to drink. Let's get real. Eleven, fourteen,
sixteen?) You don't need anyone's opinion about your
drinking! You have the freedom and the right to run your
own life, make your own decisions, do whatever you want.
It's your life, nobody controls it but you. Yeah!

All because everyone in the world thinks you should
stop drinking—screw 'em all, you will do anything you
want to do. So go ahead. Drink up.

I'm so there with you when it comes to: our right to
do, our freedom to live our own lives. I'm on the front
lines with you in defending that one!

FREEDOM . . .

We fight wars for it (well, mostly for land, religion, and
politics, but we cram it all under the heading of freedom)
. . . freedom of religion, freedom of speech, the power and
control, we so adamantly defend. It is important.

Power is important. Have you ever met anyone who likes to feel weak? I don't know too many people who would give up power, control, and freedom in their lives. If someone walked into your home and took over as if they owned it, what would you do? Fight like hell. Defend with all your might. You certainly wouldn't just hand it over. So?

Why are you?

All you have to do if you want to figure out exactly where I'm going with this is have a look back at the last few times you sat down and had a drink.

Freedom? Power? Control???

Truth be known, none of the above has anything to do with your life the minute you pick up the bottle.

!!!

I can tell you firsthand that there wasn't anything powerful about me when I was so drunk that I couldn't stand up.

There was nothing empowering about having my friends Lynann and Phyllis pick me up off the dance floor.

The conversation I had with my dad years ago, when I spent days after avoiding him like the plague because I hadn't been able to get the words out properly!?

How about that slurring, when your tongue gets thicker with every drink? There's control, huh? That's em-pow-er-ing . . .

There is nothing about alcohol that empowers. In fact, it's quite the opposite.

Let's not pretend, you and me, right here, that your right to continue to drink has anything to do with you having any power, any control, and certainly it ain't about you having freedom in your life.

Your power is gone the minute you pick up a drink.

• • •

Drinking is a power hemorrhage, and the bleeding doesn't stop when the night of drinking ends. How about that morning after???

Now there's some power. Nothing like being so sick and feeling like you are going to die!

If you've ever been hungover like I've been hungover, and I know you have, you can honestly say that it's one of the weakest positions you've ever been in.

When you can't stand the voices of the people you love most in the world because it's all just too loud? Power, control, freedom? I don't think so.

Alcohol made me feel more broken than I've ever felt in my life.

There is no power in pouring the only energy you've got into trying to get the most basic things done so you can find a place to hide till you feel better.

Having to explain what you're not even sure happened the night before (but you know it was something stupid) is a weak, weak position to be in, no matter how much you cloak it all in the "big night of drinking" humor that helps us get by.

There wasn't an ounce of power in me having to lie to my son when he so gently and lovingly came into my room to see if there was anything he could do because Mommy was feeling sick.

And Mommy lied to him.

My son with his innocence and love.

Me with my lies and disease.

My son asking questions that deepened the hole and highlighted the truth. "What's the matter, Mommy? You weren't sick last night. How'd you get so sick so fast?"

If you want to talk about moments when there is no-where to go, when the truth is blinding, this would be one of many that I can tell you from my heart—when this disease had taken every ounce of power and freedom away from me and given me nothing but a bed of lies, the deepest shame I've ever felt, and humiliation and pain, to lie in. There is nothing powerful in drinking. There is no control when you and I pick up that bottle.

One very good reason to get sober is to have real power in your life. You couldn't believe the feeling of power that goes hand in hand with being able NOT to have a drink. Every business meeting that I leave without having had the cocktail is, to this day, the greatest feeling! Knowing how not to drink—God, it's great!!! Never having to have a drink after a long day of negotiation, litigation, and organization is sooooo freeing.

When I pick my kids up after school and know that we've got the afternoon and evening to do whatever it is we want to do and there's no chance in hell that I'll be having a beer at five and be drunk by eight, that's POWER.

Power, freedom, and complete control is exactly what I felt driving home from Rusty's house after my first party without drinking. (Typical, isn't it? As soon as you stop drinking, someone you know throws a damn party and everyone, everyone is drinking!)

I'm invited, I go.

I was a little nervous. First party since I'd stopped drinking and all . . . I mean, for the last couple of years I'd gone everywhere swearing I wasn't going to drink ever again, totally committed a thousand times before, and—

bingo. "Before I knew it," I'm reaching for that beer. So? What's gonna make it different this time? All because I'm sober (whatever that meant so early on) for a week? But off I go to the party, sober and ready.

What a party, what a house, what a beautiful afternoon. That's what's running through my head for the first few minutes. Having a great sober time until about ten minutes in . . . then, I get mad. Mad at the world because I can't drink. It's the old "Everyone can, but I can't" syndrome. Even the nondrinkers. One woman I'd known for years who'd never picked up a cocktail was sucking down peach something like there was no tomorrow. They were all drinking at this fabulous, poolside, sunny-afternoon-into-the-evening, beautiful-house-in-Beverly-Hills shindig!

My idea of drinking heaven, I might add. California. Sunny. Poolside. And I'm not drinking??? Help me. Could I have picked a more difficult party to go to? (Like there would have been one that would have been easier? What? New England, forty below in the log cabin, and I wouldn't have been hankering for the hot toddy?)

The good-looking bartender, Ed—swear his name is Ed—says, "Hey, Suz, you wanna beer?"

"OH NO, ED. No thanks, really. I'll just have a soda. Peach soda."

THE OTHER HALF OF THE PEACH AND RUM NUMBER THAT EVERYONE ELSE POOLSIDE IS SUCKING DOWN.

THE NONALCOHOLIC HALF.

The peach soda half of the drink.

I hate soda and now I hated peach. Peach everything was on my shit list for life. All peaches forever. The state of Georgia next. Anything that represented peach, off my list of *be-nice-to*s forever . . . But peach soda it was in this new, not-drinking-alcohol and no-reason-to-be-at-a-poolside-party-because-I-can't-drink life o' mine, by Susan Powter.

The party is hopping, everyone is drinking up, the exotic drinks are being created and distributed left, right, and from control center, the bar.

Everyone is getting louder by the second, instant best friends are being made all around me, and I'm sober. Not drinking a thing. Sober Sue.

I didn't drink a thing that night. Stayed the whole party, had a great, great, time and an even better time when I got home. Don't even ask about the next morning.

The *Sober How* I didn't drink is simple and, believe me, something we are going to more than cover, but that's not what I want to tell you about right now.

What happened that night is such a freedom, power, and control issue (sounds like I need a little therapy), so much a *"Sober Why* you should" thing that we've gotta chat about it here and now.

Not only did I start having a great time, despite my mad-'cause-I-couldn't-drink self; I'm noticing that I'm getting better and better as the night goes on, and everyone else . . .?

My friends that I love? Getting stupider by the second. It's an amazing thing when you aren't ten sheets to the wind how much easier it is to see—Course 101 for those obnoxious nonalcoholic people who really do only have one or two drinks in a night out, but who cares about them?—how stupid this stuff makes us!

People were getting sloppy, falling in love. (How many times has that happened? Suddenly, six drinks later, you find out that you are sitting across the table from the greatest guy on the planet, only to find the next morning that some gross, half-bald, bad lover has taken his place.) Alcohol can be the hallucinogen without dropping the acid when it comes to love, friendship, commitment, and all the justifications and reasons why allll is soooo right . . . until the next day.

So let's get back to me and my party experience, shall we? By midnight I'm just beginning . . . HELLO, can anyone finish a sentence at this party? My party mates were goners. No self-righteousness involved, but I can't sit here and tell you that I wasn't truly amazed! I left the party feeling a tad better-than, free, happy . . . having had a great time. Who could have thought such a good time could be had without a drop of alcohol?

I left knowing that from now on I could be more alert, funnier, stronger, and have a better time because I didn't drink!

But it didn't end there. Never does with the night, there's always a morning after (Maureen McGovern resurrection?). I got home, took a nice long bath, planned the next morning (someone pinch me on this one), got into my jammies, lay down, and read a book . . . AFTER GOING TO A PARTY IN BEVERLY HILLS ON A SUNNY POOLSIDE AFTERNOON???

I was feeling great at one in the morning, ready for

sleep? Nothing could have prepared me for such a marvelous sense of control, freedom, and true power in my life simply because I knew the *why* and *how* of not drinking, and didn't. It was wonderful, but it didn't touch what happened the next morning. I don't think anything could have beaten what I woke up to.

NO HANGOVER.

NO SOUR STOMACH.

NO HEADACHE.

Lord help me, it was the most exciting thing I think I've ever felt. Much, much, much more fun and definitely more freeing than waking up, for the ten millionth time, sick, head exploding, cotton for saliva, hungover.

That morning I understood what sobriety and freedom have in common. If anyone thought they were free, it was me. Got my own money. My own last name. Can buy my own jewelry. Don't need a ring from you. Can go anywhere I want to, whenever I want.

Hey, I do TV, write books, am raising the greatest children on the planet. I'm independent, in control of my own life! If the world isn't my oyster, I don't know whose it is . . . Life is grand, but I can tell with everything in me that one of the most freeing, the truly wonderful, most freeing things in my life was and is . . .

Knowing that I can go to any party and not drink.
Knowing that I'm sober and that I'm going to be sober for the rest of my life. There is nothing better!
I know that I will never, ever again get behind the wheel of my car and drive drunk again. Never!

No more slurring words!
No more hangovers!
Never again will this thing control my life . . .

You want freedom, get sober.
You want magic and peace in your life, get sober.
You want control, get sober.
You want power in your own life, get sober.

What's disguising itself as your "right to"—that rising in your chest whenever you think of anyone telling you what to do, finding out about your drinking, or calling you on what you have known is a problem for a long, long time —has nothing to do with our "right to do whatever the hell we want to do." That feeling you get whenever you think of admitting what you've known forever, that you drink differently than other people, isn't denial. It's fear. You are scared like I was scared. Scared of a couple of things.

First, you are scared to death that you can't stay stopped drinking. You know you can stop. We all do.

Every time it "gets worse than you ever thought it would," what have you done?

Every morning you wake up with that horrible fear and the all too familiar "I can't believe I did that" feeling, you (just like me) quit drinking.

That's it. No more. Never again.

How many times have those words come out of our mouths?

We all quit drinking every morning after. But staying stopped?

So it's pretty understandable that you'd be afraid that

you can't stay stopped because you haven't been able to yet!

It's one big fear that we all have. And the other?

Saying the words *I'm alcoholic*. A fear otherwise known as denial? Well, is it?

It wasn't for me. I knew I was alcoholic. There was no question that my drinking was different from other people's. I'd watched my friends leave a glass of wine half full and wondered why anyone would do that. Drinking had certainly "become a problem" in my life.

You've seen the same things I saw? Drinking more and more, progression, progression, progression? Earlier and earlier in the day, not every day, but someday getting that buzz by one or two in the afternoon??? Waking up three or four mornings a week with a headache and not feeling so great? Nobody can tell me that I wasn't acutely aware of the number of times I'd told myself I wasn't going to drink that night and found myself with a beer in my hand!

I knew it. I'd seen it before and I knew what was going on.

But I didn't want to say the words I'm alcoholic. Not because I was in denial, but because we all know what happens when we do . . .

We hit a gutter.
  Go to a meeting.
  Get a sponsor.
  Do ninety meetings in ninety days.
  (All the while doing our moral inventory.)
  Apologize.

And begin our new life knowing that from now on . . .
It's an art to listen.
Easy does it is the way we live.
First things first.
We are going to *take the cotton out of our ears and put it in our mouth.*

Don't drink even if your ass falls off is our new saying for life (and what a saying it is!).

We are definitely going to *let go, let God, whatever God we choose* (the new and improved version).

We will make sure we *never get hungry, angry, lonely, and tired*—HALT.

The *Serenity Prayer* is on our bed stand forever, and from now on, for the rest of our lives, our life is to be lived *one day at a time* . . .

Admitting you are alcoholic means that from now on, for the rest of your life, you are one of them . . . the people who can't control their drinking. The ones with the problem. The ones who, for the rest of their lives, have to tag on "and I'm an alcoholic" at the end of what, for everyone else, is a simple introduction. "Hi, my name is . . ."

Not us. Not you and me. We have a different ending forever.

Why would you step into that?

And the other of the "Why would ya?" that I know you've thought about, but I'm not sure anyone has had the *cojones* to put into print, is.

Why would you ever think you could get and stay
   sober if you haven't every time you've tried?

Why wouldn't you be afraid to say the words *I'm alcoholic*. You should be, especially when you find out what's really involved in that statement! Before you make the statement, you need to understand this:

"Alcoholism is tragically and fundamentally misunderstood. Every aspect of the disease is confused, distorted by myth and misconception."

And those myths, misconceptions, and distortions about your disease absolutely affect you and your sobriety. Believe me, from the AMA to AA to the government and your neighbor, there are judgment, assumption, distortion, fear, shame, crippling ignorance (and what ignorance is powerful?) surrounding your disease that will affect your sobriety every step of the way unless you understand it and change it.

Why would you ever say the words *I'm alcoholic* when, as far back as the first century, the Roman philosopher and lawyer Seneca could pronounce, "Drunkenness is nothing but a condition of insanity purposely assumed," and, in 1980, people like former representative R. K. Dornan were still spewing junk like "[alcoholism is] an absence of self-discipline"?

I'm a wee bit (and the last time I went to Ireland was . . .?) confused, Mr. Seneca. (Is that what you call a Roman philosopher? Never slept with one of them.) Purposely assumed insanity? And Mr. Dornan . . . I happen to have a lot of self-discipline in my life. What's that got to do with the disease of alcoholism?

What does one have to do with the other? *Nothing* is the answer. But watch out, because once you speak the words *I'm alcoholic* it's not just Seneca and Dornan you're gonna have to worry about.

Wait till you hear from people (if you can call congressmen people) like Representative Samuel Devine (in a session of Congress, talking about alcohol) making statements like, "My opinion is that it is a weakness, because otherwise we could attribute all our weaknesses to disease."

Hello! Mr. Dumbo (pardon me—that would be an enormous insult to the elephant), alcoholism has been established as a physical disease since 1957. That would be thirty-nine years ago. A physical disease, not a weakness, not an absence of self-discipline. A disease . . . like heart disease, diabetes . . . disease.

Why are we talking *weakness* of anything? Alcoholics aren't alcoholics because we are weak.

Why is this thinking all over our disease? You want *whys*, big ones? I've got them for you!

If you are at all interested in where this incorrect, very damaging, terribly wrong—excuse me, purposely assumed (insane???)—thinking came from . . . all you have to do is look as far as our political leaders, like Representative H. R. Gross, making statements like "If the federal government provides funds for 'those who let themselves become victims of booze,' then it should also aid those addicted to gambling, nicotine, and Southern grits" . . . And Southern grits and the disease of alcoholism have so very much in common?

What a man, what a leader!

Mr. Morris Chafetz, director of the National Institute on Alcohol Abuse and Alcoholism says he does "not happen to believe that alcoholism is a disease."

OH, REALLY? Mr. Chafetz, you have decided that the thirty-nine years of research about my disease—what, it doesn't count?

Mr. Chafetz thinks alcoholism is "a symptom of a myriad of psychological and social problems."

Help me, Jesus!!!! Think about it. When the people in charge of our country's laws and the director of the National Institute on Alcohol Abuse and Alcoholism, who influence the general public's understanding of our disease, are making statements like this and thinking this way . . . what do you think? It's not a good beginning? Bad foundational stuff that can only get worse??? Yep, that's it. I'd say we've got a bad, bad, beginning.

Thirty-nine years of research having firmly established that you and I have a disease, and whenever the subject of alcoholism comes up you'll still hear people talking about morality, weakness of will, character flaws, and psychological problems? Starting with the boys in the government, the "alcoholism experts" laying the foundation of ignorance and incorrect information . . .

You want to know why you may not want to get up and scream, "Hi, I'm Jean, and I'm an alcoholic," to the world? Because what you may have suspected all along is true— we are not very well liked.

It's assumed that we choose to drink, so therefore we should pay.

Who had the beer before you got into the car?
Who decided to stay at the bar and drink instead
     of coming home?
Who had too much to drink and ruined the whole
     "occasion" again?

Alcoholism is not only completely misunderstood; it's
not something our society is ready to embrace, understand, or work with.

Human Behavior magazine did a study and found alcoholism and mental illness at the bottom of the list of "least
acceptables" in our world.

Guess what was more acceptable than you and I?

paraplegics and epileptics
hunchbacks
dwarfs
diabetics
amputees

Can you believe this?

What's up with that? I'd first like to say that I am going
to take the time, energy, and cash it would take to gather a
group of the other "unacceptables" from *Human Behavior*'s
little study and put together the traveling show of all time.

Check your local listings, folks, because we unacceptables
are coming to town and it's gonna be one hell of a show.

I'm assuming that the other unacceptables are as insulted
as I was when I realized what list we are on (or that we

are all on a list at all?). But remember, alcoholics are at the bottom of that list. We are the most unacceptable.

I was at my son's baseball game the other day. Moms in the stands rooting for the team, coaches on the field coaching, and one of the guys on the field was an abusive butt.

He was screaming his head off at these thirteen-year-olds, calling them idiots, telling them they sucked at the game. Let's write a whole other book on the parents in the stands that allow this abuser to abuse their children—all "in the name of the game." What do we allow in the name of the game? O. J. Simpson mean anything to anyone?

This coach was going crazy. His behavior was irrational, nuts, and completely uncalled for. Of course, everyone started talking about it, and one of the stand moms said, "Well, he's probably alcoholic"!

My ears perked up like a jackrabbit in heat (not quite sure which part of my Deep South past lives that came from) because I couldn't believe what I was hearing. So I asked what she meant.

"There's a good chance he's alcoholic because that's typical behavior for an alcoholic."

"Do you think he's drunk right now? It's ten A.M.," I asked, dying to hear the answer.

"No, no, no he doesn't have to be drunk. It's just typical of the way they act."

You gotta put this together in order to understand the full impact of her statement on my brain and body.

I'm in the stands at a ball game. Not my favorite place to be. (Love watching my sons play, but I've found over the years that the mentality in the stands of every ball game I've ever been to is something that could easily make you lose faith in the human race.) This woman is yakking on and on about the alcoholic personality. Heads are nodding, like a good sermon down South . . .

"Yes sir, that's right."

"Um, sure is . . . Yep, if that ain't so."

"Ah ha . . . yes it is . . . truth be known!"

And I'm thinking (loud enough that they all should have been able to hear me), *GOD HELP ME. This man was*—and still is, although he ain't coaching in our league anymore, thank you very much—*an abusive butt. These people all have him slotted under the title* alcoholic.

I'm there watching my sons play ball.

I do TV.

They like me a lot.

I'm responsible in their eyes.

I have a good job.

I'm normal.

And I'm alcoholic . . .

They're all sitting talking to the real thing about what we are all like, and according to them I could have blown at any moment and started abusing children!

Maybe you are chalking all this up to people-in-the-stands, overheated, one-too-many-hot-dogs thinking? Well don't, because I've got examples of that kind of ignorance coming from the brains of some of the smartest I've ever met . . . Simon & Schuster. Literary people?? You don't get fancier-schmancier than some of these very educated folks in the book world.

What's the first thing they said (a whole group of them) when they found out I was alcoholic?

"How is that possible?"

"How could she be so successful and alcoholic?"

Excuse me . . .

Winston Churchill . . . prime minister of Great Britain and a great hero *and* alcoholic?

Ulysses S. Grant . . . so let's ask him, how do you end a war and be alcoholic?

Doc Severinsen . . . so I guess we need to call him and ask how you do a historic, twenty-five-year run, one of the best shows on tele, and be a drunk?

Don Newcombe, former star pitcher for the Brooklyn Dodgers.

The Kennedys . . . just pick any one of them.

Hundreds of top athletes, from golf to baseball to hockey to the skating rink. . . . Guess what? WE ARE EVERYWHERE.

Croon and drink? Sure, it can be done. Just ask one of the best singers in the world, Bing Crosby.

Do the news, Linda Ellerbee.

Love Story and drink, Ali MacGraw.

Why would anyone still gasp, sigh, turn away when they hear the word *alcoholic*? Why is this ignorance still so pervasive? Haven't we seen enough successful, famous, well-known, respected people who are also alcoholic? One does not exclude the other. Alcoholic and successful, sure—it happens all the time. So does judgment, fear and shame. Once you say you are alcoholic, things will never be the same again, until of course we get educated and change current recovery thinking.

You bet people look at you differently when they hear you are alcoholic.

• • •

Come on, you know it . . . Don't tell me you aren't afraid of "them" finding out. Whoever "them" may be.

President of your company knows you are an alcoholic?

Other moms at the PTA know that you have a drinking problem?

Your publisher is about to sign another contract with you. What do you think? It's any different once they know you are a drunk?

Why? (See the *why* everywhere?) When it's been proven for years that

"Studies conclude that there is no evidence to support the belief that personality disorders predispose a person to alcoholism."

"When people say that someone's environment or mental or emotional problems turned them into an alcoholic, that is like saying loneliness causes syphilis."

"Physiology not psychology determines whether one drinker will become addicted to alcohol and another will not."

Alcoholics don't abuse alcohol—alcohol abuses them.

Yet the standard way of thinking is that we imbibers have chosen this evil, horrible, pleasure-filled, cup-runneth-over life, and damn it we should (if this were a movie, the mob would be coming around the bend, marching and screaming down the cobblestone streets in the old village square, ready to lynch) pay the price.

"The alcoholic is generally considered to be a moral degenerate who chooses a life of abasement and through lack of willpower and maturity allows himself to lose his job, his family, and his self-respect."

The old *you become an alcoholic* is something I hear everywhere I go—people talking about someone's drinking problem and trying to pinpoint the time that he/she became an alcoholic and what happened to make them choose drink over think . . .

> "It was just around the time that her mother died that she started drinking heavily."
> "Oh, the divorce sent him right into alcoholism."
> "As soon as she got that promotion she became an alcoholic."
> "The pressures of the job."
> "That relationship."

Recently I found myself running to the bookstore, so excited, to buy a *New York Times* best-seller, written by a female alcoholic, with a fab title, dying to read it and hear the nineties voice of the female alcoholic. I got the book, couldn't wait to crack the binding, and within minutes, hurled it across the room.

I couldn't believe the whining, the blaming, the million reasons that she gave to tell us why she was alcoholic.

Her father didn't pay enough attention to her . . . *whaaaaaaaaaa*. So she "became" an alcoholic.

Society expected too much from her as a woman, mother, wife . . . *whaaaaaaaaaa*. So she started to suck down a couple of bottles a day of anything that ignites near a flame.

Come on, spare me. The thing was unreadable. It's such a shame, it is still so pervasive—this thinking that we don't know how to love enough and that has led to . . . yadedade . . .

The truth is you have a disease. That fact has been established since 1957, but the thinking is still that alcoholism is a choice. Something drove you and me to it, and there are certain personality traits, behaviors, that pinpoint who we are. That's not true. There's no such thing as a characteristic of an alcoholic.

Alcoholism has been slightly uncloseted during the last thirty years, thanks to Mr. (OHHHHHHHHHHHHH NO!) Bill Wilson, one of the founders of AA.

But current recovery thinking still has a long, long way to go in order for you, me, and the countless number of other alcoholics to get and stay sober.

Because unless we get this weakness-of-will, morality-issue, character-defect thinking out of the disease of alcoholism, it will be another thirty-nine years before you and me and millions of others (because this disease ain't going nowhere—as long as there is alcohol, there will be alcoholics) will be able to get treatment for our disease.

We have to get to the truth now, or . . .

You will not be able to get and stay sober unless you are one of the lucky 7–12 percent (their stats, not mine) that make it in current recovery programs.

And millions of people will continue to get no treatment for a disease that not only affects those suffering but has an enormous price tag for our nation.

In order to get to the truth about alcoholism we have to start with one of the most explosive issues—alcoholic behavior.

!"|!!/

Alcoholic Behavior

What makes us drink?
Why did we become alcoholic?
Why are we irresponsible?
Why did he drive drunk?
Why don't we just quit? The *whys* behind alcoholic behavior. Irresponsible alcoholic behavior. Our characteristics. Our weakness, if you will power (little play with words), otherwise known as our behavior.

What comes first, the chicken or the egg?

Alcoholics are severely judged by their behavior. Remember, we are probably violent, definitely irresponsible, so weak-willed we just can't seem to get a grip. We have the self-discipline of a jellyfish (sea amoebas and me, tight as they get). We are all these things, and that's why we drink?

Right from the Big Book we are told:

Our (your and my) willpower is practically nonexistent.

We are "such unfortunates, and are naturally incapable of grasping and developing a manner of living which demands rigorous honesty," that . . .

We (you and I) "cannot manage our own lives."

Is that why we drink irresponsibly?
Or—WE DRINK, LIKE THE REST OF THE WORLD DOES, AND WE BECOME ALL THESE THINGS . . . AHHHHHHHHHHHHHHHHHHH!

Here we go. Hang on tight, because we are about to get into some heavy-duty "murky" white-water rafting. This is where staunch recovery people really get mad and pull out all the low-rent sober stops.

It's here in our *sober why* discussion that you can expect protests, yelling, screaming, and mad, mad, mad . . . because when it's even suggested that alcohol creates the behavior that we are so arrested, tried, and convicted by, it makes people nuts. It cracks the foundation of the recovery community. It puts a whole lot of people—their jobs, egos, and reputations—on the line (and those boys in Congress don't like that). It exposes your doctor's complete ignorance and ability to do anything about the 22 million alcoholics in this country that desperately need treatment. It spotlights AA's involvement in the ignorance of current recovery thinking and their desire to stay there . . . It basically blows the whole damn thing to pieces.

But we gotta do it if you want the answer to why you have been so afraid to say the words *I'm alcoholic.*

. . .

Bad behavior isn't the cause of our drinking. We don't drink because we are running from some emotional problem. Our drinking has nothing on the planet to do with not being able to handle our lives. Our emotions and our alcoholic drinking don't have anything to do with each other as the cause for alcoholism. They certainly are tied together by the time this disease gets you by the throat, but our bad, impaired judgment, stupid decisions, fear, lying, shame, hiding are all the *consequences* of our disease.

Like the attack of the heart for the heart patient, our behavior comes with the disease.

It's as inevitable as the rolls on the stomach of the person who eats a ton of fat and doesn't exercise.

No different from the seizure of the diabetic, who hasn't managed his or her disease.

It comes with it . . . part and parcel . . . a given . . . the inevitable.

Facts are:

"Alcoholism is known to be a true physical disease which transforms its victims leaving them with little or no control over their behavior."

"In medical language I consider drunkness to be a disease produced by remote cause and giving birth to actions that disorder the functions of health."

"[Alcoholics] are ill and victims of chemical changes they cannot control."

"Personality changes are a result of alterations in normal brain chemistry caused by heavy drinking.**"**

But the "current-beneath-the-surface" thinking about alcoholism is that there are certain types, behavioral similarities, certain personalities, etc., that create the alcoholic, cause alcoholism, or can explain the reason the drinking got soooo very out of control.

I was with someone the other day, a wonderful woman (a friend, very, very educated, unbelievably involved in the recovery community), a major speaker in AA all over L.A. (Listen to how that sounds—AA, L.A., AA, L.A. So? Why did I even bring that up? Who knows? But onward . . .) Both of us are forty-plus women (that's not a size, that's an age), support ourselves. She's been enormously successful, she's bright, funny, and charming (I'd say we have a lot in common so far? Joking!), and we are both alcoholics.

She has handed her power over, knows that she will meet for the rest of her life, has surrendered to such a high power, don't ask!

We are both alcoholic and we think differently about recovery. She knows how strongly I feel about the importance of biochemical support during recovery and my beliefs that the treatment for the disease of alcoholism should be available to everyone suffering.

But, remember we are both such Cosmo, nineties women who are interested in opening the gateways of communication in recovery and getting people what they need to stay sober. SO, FINE. That's it. Not a problem. We've had twelve thousand conversations and never a moment of anything but love and respect till the other day, when one statement, one damn statement, created more tension than all twelve thousand conversations we've had in the past combined could have ever created.

My friend was talking about alcoholics and she said, "You know the typical characteristics of an alcoholic behavior."

And I said, "There is no such thing as typical characteristics of alcoholic behavior."

FROZEN . . .

Such tension you couldn't imagine. She was pissed (not drunk—mad). She couldn't believe that I could make a statement like that.

We had our moment. I wasn't budging (and neither will you once you've got the information that I've got). She made a face that made it clear that she was going to "tolerate" my comment and let it slide by for whatever reason.

I walked away fascinated at the power of this one thing, "The Behavior-of-an-Alcoholic Discussion." The one that gets us into issues like

Why "we" choose to drink.
Why "we" let it get out of control.
What's wrong with us that isn't wrong with people
    who can control their drinking?
How did it happen?
Why can't he just come home at night instead of
    going out and drinking?
What would make her think she could get into that
    car and drive after having had so many drinks?
Who would ever, ever drink with a new baby?
Oh, my God, how could they?

The best place for me to speak from, right now, is my own.

I am not an irresponsible human being. But I've done things drunk that are incredibly irresponsible.

I believe driving drunk is wrong. I would never, ever, ever put anyone in danger . . . except after a few beers.

Here's what I am. I'm a mother, a writer, an alcoholic, a businesswoman, a friend, a daughter, an alcoholic, a sister, an alcoholic . . . I am all those things. One of which is an alcoholic.

Nobody made that more clear to me than Rusty during one of our discussions about shame. The shame I used to feel about "having this thing," being an alcoholic! Maybe the same shame you feel at "just not being able to handle it?"

Well, whenever I'd get the horrible sick feeling I used to get . . . (I still do once in a while. The other day I'm unpacking a box—just moved, you know, and dying is easier than moving a home and a family—and came across a tape of a party that I went to when I was still drinking. I almost puked. Didn't feel too much better two years later than I did when I put the tape away and chose not to think about it. OH HOW MUCH FUN WRITING THIS BOOK CAN BE AT TIMES!)

When I think back on some of the things "I did" that were so stupid and put sooo much at risk, it takes just seconds to get right back to feeling like a complete idiot. How could I have acted that way??? The deep, deep shame that's connected to drunk behavior can be conjured up in seconds. It's all easy to do because drunk behavior is stupid behavior.

It was Rusty who cleared it all up for me. When I told her how I was feeling, she said: "Susan, you are the farthest thing from an idiot. You couldn't be an idiot if you tried. You are smart, you are funny, you are talented, you are the best mother, you are a wonderful friend. You are no idiot."

Isn't it lovely to have someone who knows you so well? (Just a joke again.)

I thanked her—prematurely, because she was in the beginning of her next sentence by the time the *thanks* came out of my mouth.

She's saying, "But you drunk? OH, MY GOD, you're a fool!!!"

OK, drunk behavior is stupid behavior. I'm there and ready to take full responsibility.

"You are one of the smartest people I've met, but when you are drinking, you are stupid. Yeah, I'd say drinking makes you stupid, Susan!"

OUCH! Tough love can hurt (probably why they call it tough), but I can take it.

"It made you KINDA gooney . . ."

Thanks for coming, Rus. Now, about that meeting I'm sure you have to get to right away . . .

"You make stupid decisions because it isn't you making them. It's the alcohol, that beast, the monster that takes over your body. You look stupid, you act stupid, you say stupid things . . ."

All righty, Rus, appreciate it, talk to ya soon . . . Get outta here, you sponsor, you!

YUUUUUUUUUUUUUUUUUUUUUUUUCK, but true!

• • •

You don't drink because you are a bad person, or because you have certain emotional characteristics (although you've got a few physical characteristics of your disease—we all do), and you certainly don't drink because you can't manage your life.

You don't want to drive drunk, but you do.

It isn't you that is a slurring, sloppy fool. It's you drunk.

You may be an idiot sober. If so, you can bet your ass that you are a bigger idiot drunk.

If you drunk is a caricature of yourself, then alcohol would be the artist with the pen in its hands, drawing a distorted, cartoon version of who you really are.

"Studies conclude that there is no evidence to support the belief that personality disorders predispose a person to alcoholism."

Our personality changes as a result of drinking, not the other way around.

I didn't start drinking because I have some personality flaw; I started drinking because who doesn't?

Unless you live in an Amish community, who the hell doesn't start drinking in junior high, high school, or college, all depending on how socially queer you are? If you are really out there, it's in your early twenties, but most of us (the hip ones?) start drinking much, much earlier than our twenties. And anyway, it doesn't matter when you first take that sip of whiskey—the point is, we all do. And we all know why. It's pretty obvious how much campaigning, encouragement, and "good times ahead" advertising gets drilled into our brains since jump street . . . and when you understand the power of the alcohol boys, you'll understand why we are getting the messages we are getting, messages interpreted by *Dateline, Time* magazine, and Linda Ellerbee (worship her).

It's the new thing, you know. Cover of *Time*. Every news magazine show. The topic of the day is addiction: What's the problem? How does "it" happen?

It floors me that in this day and age we spend an hour of national television time, network time worth millions, to ask the dumbest questions, which get us nowhere, which do nothing but feed the ignorance.

Here's what I just watched on three top programs . . .

Highlight a bunch of college kids.

Everyone drinks.

Everyone parties.

But something happens to Bobby.

They interview Bobby's parents. Nice, normal, white. "What went wrong?" is the focus for the first fifteen minutes.

Interview Bobby's friends and try and find out what about Bobby's "personality" told you something was wrong.

Did you see the "behavior" changes?

Why Bobby?

What's wrong with Bobby?

No mention of any physical disease.

Never a mention that Bobby was the only one, in a group of ten, that got addicted to alcohol, and why.

Treatment? Never even thought about.

Just focus on what went wrong—in the family, with his upbringing. Pressure at school. Bobby's inability to handle —what? Handle everything.

Bobby couldn't handle; therefore, he drank!!!

You wanna know why Bobby drank (since that's all we seem to be focused on)? I'll tell ya why. For the same reason we all start drinking.

We start drinking the minute we can get our hands on the stuff because it's the coolest thing you can do according to everything we see and hear. And when you and I did something different happened to you and me.

The question of the recovery hour needs to be, why did something different happen to me, or Bob, or Jenny, or all the other alcoholics out there? And it ain't just me, Bob, or Jenny that has to get the answer.

This book isn't written just for alcoholics and people who love them. It's written for the United States government, our educational system, the AMA, the insurance companies, AA, every hospital, juvenile delinquent center, and prison out there . . . because this disease does not affect just us, it affects every single human being living in this country. And here's how.

Child abuse	in 60 percent of cases reported, alcohol was involved
Rape	in 40 percent of cases reported, alcohol was involved
Fatal Accidents	in 65 percent of cases reported, alcohol was involved

Suicide   in 80 percent of suicide victims had been drinking

We don't have a choice but to understand what is happening in the chemically altered brain of every drinking alcoholic in this country. We have to learn about what's going on inside the physically ill body of everyone who is suffering with this disease, and treat it.

Just a thought, and maybe a piece of the big, big puzzle that we all feel completely overwhelmed by so much of the time when we look at the news, hear about the young children dying in the accident, or hear about the malicious crime that has no rhyme or reason!

The truth about alcoholic behavior is . . .

Our behavior is affected by this disease because of our hurting brains.

What? Because you wear a business suit your behavior wasn't affected by your alcoholism? Mine was. I'm not a liar, and I lied. I would never, ever drive drunk and put my children and everyone else on the road in danger, but I did.

And the irresponsible behavior that happens on whatever level it happens on soaks into our hearts and souls and makes us feel bad, like bad people, and what is offered as "recovery" makes us feel completely incapable of handling our own lives.

The worse the behavior, the worse you feel about yourself. The longer it continues—the further you get away from the original you—the more you become the alcoholic, sick, diseased, deteriorating, both emotionally and physically. That can and must change.

Why wouldn't you be afraid of saying the words *I'm alcoholic?*

Maybe now that you understand that the government, current recovery thinking, and society doesn't like you, and isn't going to tolerate you, and that there is nothing being done to help you get treatment for, a cure for, a solution for the disease that you are suffering from . . . maybe now you'll join those of us who are interested in getting the truth out and getting treatment.

Anyone who's ever grown up in an alcoholic home, anyone who is alcoholic and done any research at all knows that this thing runs in families. Trace it back. Just look over your shoulder. If you are alcoholic, there's a very, very good chance that there isn't a generation in the leaves of your family oak where you won't find a good old uncle, cousin, brother, father who just couldn't control himself. If you're coming from an alcoholic family it's never, ever too difficult to find someone who was a guaranteed "three sheets to the wind" whenever alcohol was around.

If you look just a little harder you'll hear rumors of the crazy aunt, sister, mother, or any other female relative that had a "condition." A nervous condition. Spent a lot of time in bed. Couldn't go out much. You know . . .

You won't hear detailed war stories about her because (up until yesterday) there was still an enormous amount of shame connected to being female and alcoholic. Eyes look away, cheeks blush, and sad sighs were connected to the unsaid message: old Aunt Jane was hitting the bottle!

Uncle Drunk was (and is) treated very differently than Aunt Drunk, no question about it.

To this day, if you tell your friends a story of someone at the party slurring words, acting really stupid, loud, obnoxious . . . tell 'em it was Bob and you'll get,

"God, poor guy. He gets like that all the time." "That's just Bob. You invite him, you gotta deal with him, help the poor guy out."

Tell 'em it was Sue and you'll hear,

"She is so gross. Every time she comes she acts so stupid and slutty."

Tell 'em Sue is a mother of three and you'll hear, "Those poor children, having a mother like that."

All you have to do is grow up in an alcoholic home, like the 55 million kids who are living in alcoholic homes in this country today, to know without a shadow of a doubt that this thing is handed down. But it's been pooh-poohed by the "experts" forever. Why? Why no acknowledgment, boys?

The big argument for years has been that we learned (behavioral, environmental—anything but genetic) to drink because we grew up in alcoholic homes. That's why everyone in our families (going back ten generations?) is alcoholic. There's that behavior spotlight again.

In order to bust open the heredity-behavior argument and get the information you need, you need to understand the answer to the question that we all have—

WHY ME?
Why did this "happen" to me?

• • •

Do you want to know? Its simple.

CONSPIRACY. It's a conspiracy.

|"!/

I know what you're thinking. You're thinking it's time to close the book real slow, put it down and walk away real quietlike, get far away from any connection with this ex–fat woman and drunk who's talking about some kind of conspiracy—carefully, quietly, and as if you never, ever picked up the book in the first place. Are you sure, at this point, that I'm a stalker kook?

OK, I'll tell ya what. You read what I found out and you tell me what you think. We'll see, at the end of this little discussion, if you don't see the answer to the biggest of the big *why* questions—why has it all been allowed???

Conspiracy!

Listen, it's not so far-fetched. We've seen it happen before. In fact, we are right in the middle of it happening.

You tell me . . .

An industry that has killed millions?

An industry that has lied through its teeth in order to make billions?

An industry that preys on the young and gets them hooked at the earliest age?

No, it's not the Catholic Church we are talking about (although . . .), it's the tobacco industry.

They knew, in the fifties, that the product they spent millions glamorizing killed. There was no question then, and there's no question some forty-plus years (and how many deaths?) later that the tobacco boys were sell, sell, selling a product that was directly connected to heart disease, stroke, lung cancer, asthma, emphysema, and God knows what else. But we got educated. (Not that we came along peacefully. What it took for fabulous people like Ralph Nader and Tony Randall—sure, I remember him talking about how disgusting ciggies were years ago on national tele, and they called him picky and annoying and laughed!)

The American Cancer Society, the American Heart Association, the American Lung Association, and a bunch of English physicians have worked for almost three decades to do the very same thing we are doing right now— get the truth exposed and let you make up your own mind. That's what happened with the tobaccy boys. They got uncovered and the consumer got (and is getting) smarter and smarter and smarter.

Dying for an industry's profits is something we are less willing to do. My sons' awareness about smoking is totally different than mine was at their age. They know it's a dirty, deadly, disgusting (the three D's) habit.

My thirteen-year-old son says:

"People who smoke are dumb because they are hurting themselves. Shortening their lives. It smells dirty and it's stupid!"

And my fourteen-year-old:

"Smoking is really annoying. It fills the room and takes away my air."

How's that for genius? Beautiful and brilliant, what a burden!

I was smoking at eleven and thought it was the icy-est of coolest things to do. One generation apart, and a totally different understanding and respect—the truth versus the hype! Amazing and bravo to everyone who dragged us to this place of awareness, because it wasn't easy. Those tobacco boys are mighty powerful boys. Lots of cash, lots of political clout, lots and lots of influences in the direction they want things to go. How do you think things went their way (despite all the death and disease that was directly connected to the product they were making billions from) for forty-five years?

Now it's changing and they are being gently hand-slapped. (Still a lot of government apologizing to the tobacco boys going on. It's a difficult place Congress is in. There's no more denying. We know too much to veil it. And one of their biggest political cash contributors is pipe-smoking mad.)

Yes, it's a powerful bunch, those tobacco boys, but they ain't nothing compared to the alcohol boys. Nothing! A pimple on the face of the elephant . . . My God, once you understand the power these boys have, you'll be able to make the connection between the misinformation we are getting, the recovery standards that are not being set, laws swaying public opinion the way it is being swayed, your disease and the treatment that ain't happening and why . . . the big *why, oh why.*

And it all starts with the cash. It's not such a bubble buster anymore, this policy decision making for loads and loads of profit that our government is steeped in.

We know too well that billions of dollars' worth of profits plays a huge part in things happening that shouldn't. Money, money, money and lots of it is the reason why soooooo much is not seen, so much is passed through, and more than you and I could imagine is covered up and allowed!

No real reason to go into all the pollution, destruction,

waste, death (but twist my arm) that has been allowed, passed through, OK'd, covered up in our world. It's being done with your food, your air, your water, your money, your everything—and it's being done with your disease.

The laws that are being passed, the policy on alcoholism in our country that is being pushed, the thinking that is interfering with you getting treatment are being established by:

a. the president of the United States
b. our senators and congressmen on Capitol Hill
c. the alcohol lobbies
d. the hospitality industry

Lobbyists get to the president by doing the same thing that everyone that wants to get into your pants does—wine and dine ya!

A couple of years ago there was Wine Appreciation Week. The wine boys visited the president. Talk came up about the taxes that were about to be raised on wine.

Interesting that that would come up at a dinner with the wine boys and the president?

The wine boys didn't think that wine should be taxed the way it was about to be taxed because wine is an "agricultural product, not a sin." (Hello! What does that have to do with anything???)

So they chatted, and guess what? By the end of the week America got a new message . . . You've heard it. GREAT NEW NEWS IN THE LAND.

WINE IS GOOD FOR YOU. HAVE YA HEARD?

Something in red wine is stopping the French from dropping like flies.

Something in wine has something to do with preventing heart disease (though nobody can really tell you why).

New message in the land . . . moderate alcohol consumption is good for your heart!

See how it works? Getting the picture? One hand feeds the other. Friends helping (wink, wink) friends. Everyone sleeping with everyone (kind of like the Kennedy administration). Lots of support for presidential campaigns from friends like August Busch (that's not the name of a hedge in the Hamptons, it's the head of Anheuser-Busch), who helped finance President Clinton's inauguration . . . You know, the big, big, big expensive party a couple of years back? Where do you think those Clydesdales came from?

And August's other job? What's he up to? Busy serving on the president's economic-policy council.

Yep, he's right there helping decide the economic policies of our country.

Probably has no problem being completely objective?! Wouldn't you say?

Two and a half million jobs gone if beer doesn't get brewed!

Taxes—billions—*vámonos* if we don't buy the stuff.

Thousands of businesses out of business . . .

Ever thought where all those aluminum cans come from?

Advertisers that advertise what's in those cans?

The restaurants who survive by bar business alone?

Newspapers, magazines would have huge holes were those Absolut ads gone.

I'm sure none of it gets in the way when there is a decision to be made by the men with the last names of . . . Anheuser and Busch?

Power? Cash? Influence? Sway? Cajole? Manipulate?

Mr. Big at Seagram's was power lunching with the president recently (after having just contributed $1.5 million to his campaign), and soon after, guess what disappears? Not the saltshaker, but the liquor-taxes discussion, from the upcoming health care financing discussion. Amazing, isn't it?

This is an industry, my friends, that contributed $6 million to the president's campaign last year . . . What? Someone gives you $6 million to get done what you want to get done, and what are you gonna do, kick 'em in the teeth? Don't think so. That's not the way it works in this world.

Listen, I'm not the one to pick up the rock in this glass house. All you gotta do is throw me a compliment and I'll marry you! Don't tell me I won't compromise. You don't even have to contribute $6 million to my campaign. I've signed my life away for a whole lot less than that. So who can blame the president?

It's a very tangled, complicated web that's been woven by the liquor boys, and not one that is gonna get untangled anytime soon. The cashola being thrown around, the boys sucking up to the boys, lots and lots of profit on the line, and it's endless. Our senators and congressmen are nothing more than the food in the web, and believe me, there's plenty for the fly to eat!

!!!

You may think that what's happening in Congress has nothing to do with you, the hangover you are dealing with, the shame and fear you are living in, the disease you are suffering from, but it does. What's happening in the halls of Congress, at the powerful lunch and dinner tables all over this country, and in our government has everything on earth to do with you getting healed.

You see, it's the fly-food boys who are deciding which laws are passed or rejected. They set the tone for the nation's response to your disease. It's them that create the public awareness or lack of it about alcoholism. If you are looking for answers to *why,* you gotta start here, because this, my friends, is where it all begins.

Tax increase or decrease, it's them.

Research to be done or not done on alcohol, it's them.

Advertise anywhere they want—no restrictions—it's them.

Where it's sold, how it's sold, to whom it's sold, it's them . . .

You want an example of what's happening that's directly connected to you and your drinking? Check out the craziness around the new-and-improved, trying-to-get-passed-but-has-no-chance-in-hell-of-happening blood-alcohol-level law.

For the past couple of years, there has been some

heavy-duty fighting going on in Congress. The momentum is building for support to lower the blood-alcohol-level standard for drivers. Meaning, drink less and busted more easily.

They don't want it to happen because:

Wholesalers wouldn't sell as much.

Retailers will be feeling it.

Restaurants will be losing their biggest profits.

Campaign dollars aren't going to be quite as much.

Advertising budgets cut, cut, cut.

The bottle and aluminum boys are going to have to fill their product with something else.

All hell breaks loose.

So the lobbyists lobby. Do you know what that means? I didn't till I started doing this research, because, quite honestly, who cares?

A lobbyist is an individual who is hired by another individual, group, organization, or government to promote the agenda of those that he or she (let's get real, how many she-lobbyists are there?) reflects.

A lobbyist is often an attorney (that's always a good sign?) or a public relations agency (both of whom you can guarantee will tell the truth?) that will pressure congressmen and senators to defeat legislation that does not support their cause. These boys are paid well to knock down everything and anything in the way of the $100 billion business that they represent. ALCOHOL. What do you think their tactics are gonna be? Fair? For the people? Interested-in-the-health-of? Get the hell out of here.

So of course the government is involved, very, very

involved, in keeping the whiskey flowing. Where would the Kennedys be without it? And here's how it's done without it looking like anything wrong is being done . . .

The current president of the Beer Institute (now there's a school I wouldn't mind going to) served in Congress for twelve years on the revenue-raising House Ways and Means Committee. Tax measures get introduced in the House.

NEON SIGN FLASHING—$7.5 BILLION IN TAXES COLLECTED ANNUALLY FROM THE SALE OF ALCOHOL.

And how are you going to vote if you were, are, or could be the president of the Beer Institute?

The president of the wholesalers (who sell the alcohol to the retailers) spent six terms in the House of Representatives, and whenever the subject of alcohol or anything surrounding it came up, which way do you think he voted??

Keep the emphasis on our behavior. Our weakness of will. Our inability to lead honest lives and make the responsible choice in our lives—AND take the focus off . . . ???

There is more involved than you or I could ever fathom in making sure that the disease of alcoholism continues to be seen as a psychological problem. Our problem. Your inability to handle your life. Because as long as it is, the industry that is profiting from the death and destruction of this disease doesn't have to answer for what they are doing . . . Again I ask you, tobacco industry mean anything to you?

The president, Congress, senators . . . very, very incestuous, and like any good inbreeding situation, there's always a cousin marrying a cousin, and it ain't no different when it comes to the perception of our disease.

There happens to be a very special cousin that everyone wants to marry in the business of keeping the truth about our disease hidden, and her name is Madison. Cousin Madison Avenue!

The Advertising Industry:

Last year $600 million was spent in liquor advertisements alone. Guess who the biggest client on Madison Avenue is? Give ya a hint. First name is Dom, last name is Pérignon.

Here's the message we get from Cousin Madison . . .

Let the good times roll, and there's only one way to do it!!!

Alcohol is

fun
exciting
refreshing
relaxing
sexy

It makes you the best you can be . . . because . . .
"I love ya, man . . . this Bud's for you!"

Spuds McKenzie . . . (Isn't that dog dead yet? . . . Actually, he is. It isn't Spuds but Spuds Jr. that's all over the beer ads now.) In the eighties Spuds was dancing around on a beach doing the eighties thing. In the nineties, the dog is still the life of the party.

He's the party animal and they love him, man!!!

• • •

Those frogs.

Those alligators.

Those fun times . . .

Those mountain-climbing boys who'll do anything, including strip in Arctic temperatures, for one thing. A beer.

Now there's common sense!

Cousin Madison has it's way, and how creative they can be! Have you seen the Xerox machine that spits out beer? All you have to do is press the start button and you've got yourself a drink. Top dollar is paid to the creative genius who thought that up.

You and I know good and well that there just is no other way to have fun on the beach!

"It doesn't get any better than this."

You know what weekends were made for . . . Michelob!

Who's this Bud for? You. And why? For all you do.

Don't ever forget: "Life is rough so your tequila shouldn't be."

Reality-check time. You've got Madison Avenue with the power of tele, ads, magazine, radio, billboards, dancing bottles of vodka, and their $600-million-a-year (plus some mighty fine perks) budget, screaming the message they want you to get. And? You have organizations like MADD, Mothers Against Drunk Drivers; SADD, Students Against Drunk Drivers; the Center for Responsive Politics; and the Center for Science in the Public Interest. And their budget? What message has a better chance of getting through?

And can you blame them for glorifying it? I mean, after all, what are they going to do, tell the truth?

When it's between the pretty people on the beach and someone heaving their guts up?

Mountain climbing, or blacking out (wouldn't be difficult to show: blank screen and a whole lot of static when you come to)—which would you pick if your paycheck came from the liquor boys? The truth or the glamorization?

Who's brave enough to stand up and shout that the $100-billion-a-year alcohol industry is also . . .

The number one killer of young adults in our country.

I got one for ya. Get the cameras. Slow roll into the preemie nursery . . . incubators, tubes going, everything, into the tiniest body you've ever seen. THE NUMBER ONE CAUSE OF MENTAL RETARDATION IN OUR CHILDREN: FETAL ALCOHOL SYNDROME. Mean anything to you? Advertise that in the middle of your football game!!!

I don't think so . . .

It's a complicated web, and we've only gone as far as the halls of Congress and the American government, which is crystal clear and pure as can be compared to some of the special-interest groups and organizations that are involved in keeping the disease of alcoholism from being treated and dealt with. You want web, you want flies, you want messy, messy, knotted and tangled like you've never? Check out the hospitality industry.

¡!!!

Yeah, hospitable . . . hospitality. Come on in (to every bar, casino, hotel, resort, nightclub) and have a good time.

You want to talk billions and billions of dollars, this would be an industry to talk it in!

Tied in to our government?

The National Restaurant Association and the food and beverage boys contributed $5 million in 1996 to presidential campaigns. You tell me.

And one more thing.

When you think casino, bar, nightclub? What group do you most closely associate to them? Do the letters *M-O-B* mean anything to you??

You got a couple of people in Congress like Senator Wellstone and Representative Ramstad who are trying to pass legislation that will curb the damage the liquor industry is doing. And then you have the hospitality industry. An industry that makes billions and is going to make sure that Representative Ramstad and Senator Wellstone never see the light of day when it comes to their little laws.

Who do you think has a better chance, Representative Ramstad, or the Mafia? Senator Wellstone, or Jimmy the Goon?

You see what we have here is a whole lot of people who make a whole lot of money.

You don't think you are up against something big?

Why? You wanted a *why . . . sober why?* I think you just got one big one with the whole conspiracy thing, and I don't even have to ask what you think, 'cause I already know. Who could read what you just read and not be completely clear about the conspiracy!!! It's a big *why,* there's no question about that, but it isn't the biggest of the *sober why*'s.

!!!!

The biggest of the *sober why*'s is the question, why would you in your wildest dreams really ever think you could get and stay sober when what's offered, when you go for help yourself or are sent by the judge, a friend, employer, intervention, or counselor . . . what do you get?

AA. Alcoholics Anonymous. The current recovery model that has a monopoly on the recovery world.

It's a good thing. It's helped 12 percent of the population. But there are 88 percent that don't make it. I've seen the support—I have been a recipient of the support: remember those wonderful women who came to my house —they were followers of AA.

The love, devotion, dedication, and persistence of some of the members of AA that I've met are admirable and truly a blessing for the 12 percent (AA success statistic) who "make it." My question is, what about the 88 percent that don't "make it"?

You want one of the biggest *sober why*'s, the final *sober why* . . . the "Why would you ever think you could get and STAY sober?" when here's what happens when you do go for help . . . You are about to get it.

You may have gone to an AA meeting. I knew I couldn't keep having private meetings forever—I mean, really, how unrealistic would that be? (although I must admit it was a thought)—and I knew I was alcoholic and wanted desperately to get sober. So what do you do?

Right, I went to a meeting. A regular AA meeting. It's hard to explain the mixture of pride, fear, ego, fear, self-loathing that was mixed together in my brain and my heart that night, but go I did, because I didn't know what else to do! That's what you do when you want to get sober? You go to an AA meeting and start doing the steps. It's all that's offered, so there I was.

The first OH-SO-HARD-TO-GET-PAST-DON'T-ASK issue, for me, was having short white hair and having been on TV. Nothing anonymous about me!

I was scared sick literally when I asked Rusty to go with me to this meeting. I thought I was going to choke on the drive there, and when we finally found the house and pulled into the parking space, got out to go in, I wasn't sure my legs would carry me. Yuck, I didn't feel good. But I went.

Walking in the door was horrible and was made even worse by a woman who walked right up to me and said, "HEY, SUSAN POWTER! OH, MY GOD, I WORK FOR ONE OF YOUR LAWYERS."

As God is my witness, I wanted to die.

At the time I was in the middle of that lawsuit with my ex- (I'm thrilled to say) partner. And I was in communication with this particular lawyer daily. Now that the minute I'd walked in the door I'd been anonymously—"Hey, Susan"—introduced, not because I ever wanted to know this woman but because we were both alcoholic and at a meeting . . . HELP ME!!!

What was I supposed to do? Every time I walked into my lawyer's office, give a nod to my new friend in sobriety??? . . .

I had visions of a secret wink.

A smirk.

A special sign to show her that I hadn't gotten drunk the night before.

My new sober pal, who I hated, that screamed my name out at the top of her lungs at an anonymous meeting of alcoholic people!

My new sober best friend, whether I liked it or not . . . What a beginning!

Thank God someone started talking. People started sitting. We gathered in the backyard-porchy kind of thing, and the meeting got under way. I was too shaken to move for a long, long time—except when I had to (I'm talking being more nervous than you've ever been in your life, including having birthed two ten-pound babies. Ladies, you know what that does to a bladder . . . I'm talking HAD to) get up to use the bathroom.

Someone was talking about being grateful to the group for something and I decided it was a good time to quietly get up and tiptoe (in five-inch heels) around the back, through the house, to the bathroom. I tap Rusty on the arm, whisper that I'll be right back, and get up to tiptoe.

I'm tiptoeing.

Pretending to listen.

Dying inside.

Nervous, frightened, hating the whole experience.

And then it happened.

The thing that made me more unanonymous than my new sober friend could ever have—I bang into (that's not bang ON, that's BANG INTO) the screen door. Straight into. Loud enough for the whole group (fifty women?) to turn around to see what the hell was going on near the entrance of the house. Who on earth was making the racket that interrupted the person who was telling her story of drinking and what it had done to her life?

OH, please, Jesus, take me now . . .

Who knows what I said as I stood staring—with a screen door imprint in the middle of my forehead (swear) —at the group, trying to explain the racket . . . ?

I don't have a clue what I said.

Excuse me.

I'm an ass.

I want to kill myself.

But I do remember looking at Rusty and knowing that she understood exactly how stuck I was at that very moment in my life, face into the screen of a door that most people would have known to open before trying to get through, with fifty alcoholic women looking at that short white-haired lady who does TV, writes books, does seminars . . . is a fitness expert and a drunk!

Please. I know I don't live in a war zone. I am aware that my life is better than half the people's on the planet and that I'm lucky to be alive, the gift of healthy children and all, but at that moment, I promise you—freezing to death in an Arctic plane crash would have felt better and been a kinder way to die than the screen mark on my face.

The rest of the meeting was a blur until I finally knew that I could get the hell out of there. It's over, thanks, let's go . . .

I'm avoiding the woman who screamed my name when I first walked in. (She had come up to me during one of the breaks with one great big "I'm-so-sorry-it-dawned-on-

me-how-wrong-identifying-you-like-that-was-could-you-
ever-find-it-in-your-heart-to-forgive-me?" kind of thing.
*Very nice, but no chance—absolutely not, never, ever will I
forgive you as long as I live. I hate you,* is what I was thinking.
But smile and nod I did, conjuring up all the convent
training of my past.) All I was focusing on was smiling,
doing the thank-you-very-much-for-having-me crap, being
as polite as my frozen mind and body could allow, walking
through all the right and polite things to say, just so I
could get the hell out of there.

As I ran/walked toward the car the woman who invited
me, and a couple of women who hadn't invited me came
and asked me what I thought of the meeting.

I told her/them the truth.

"I so very much appreciated the wonderful women
who shared their stories, their pain, their sobriety.

"The stories of courage, truth, acknowledgment that I
heard touched me deeply"—this is exactly what I said—
"and I appreciate the warmth and love from all the women
who were there. But there were some things that I didn't
understand, that I was uncomfortable with . . ." At this
point I started to cry.

Standing on the sidewalk in front of three strangers
crying is not a comfortable place for me, it's not something
I usually do, and wasn't the way I wanted to end this
fiasco, but I continued . . .

The Christian theme of the thing didn't sit well with
me. That doesn't mean I'm a devil worshiper, but all the
other religions (as much as the born-againers want to believe that they are the only ones, they are not) of the world
will understand what I'm saying when I say that the whole

white Christian theme may not be what you believe in and want to have shoved down your throat.

I had a problem with the "Our Father, who art in heaven" thing—I was raised in a Catholic convent. I've heard that one too many times.

And . . . surrender didn't sit well with me. I didn't understand it. The *I am powerless* was really something I didn't understand and was having trouble with . . . and I ended, in tears, with, "But I'm really scared because I have the feeling that if I can't just come here and accept all this stuff without question then I'll have nowhere to go and this thing will kill me."

What do you think? A warm moment among women on that sidewalk after the meeting? Tender, loving, nurturing response to what I'd said?

Nope.

The minute the words came out of my mouth the stranger who followed the lady who'd invited me, the stranger who was not invited, the woman who I didn't know and didn't want to know, pointed her finger at me and said:

"Then, sister, you may as well go drink and use tonight, because until you *surrender* and *understand that you are powerless,* you can't and won't ever get help—you'll never be sober!"

Silence.

Amazing!!!

Can't imagine it ever happening?

Well, get ready, because it does all the time . . .

Rusty was shocked. I was angry, humiliated, and steeped in all my reasons why this bullshit wasn't for me, sticking psychic voodoo pins in this mean, hateful woman, this horrible human being.

And if that was sober, HA!

You could say I was feeling a whole lot of things, but one thing I wasn't feeling was surprised. I'd seen this kind of evangelical, self-righteous attitude among program members before—remember, been there since I'm eleven. Rusty hadn't. She couldn't believe what had just happened, and her comment as we were driving away—"The first thing I'd do after an experience like that is drink a beer"—hit the nail on the head, because if I ever wanted a drink . . .

I knew firsthand, way before the angry woman's finger shaking, that the members of AA have become an unruly mob. Not quite what their founder had in mind.

How unusual—the original idea starts out right and people spoil it. How many times has that happened? Have a look at every organized religion under the sun.

I've got an angry-mob scene on tape because I did a show on alcoholism (while I was a drinking alcoholic) with an audience full of AAers and J. Mathews Larson, Ph.D., the woman who wrote one of the best books out there on alcoholism, *Seven Weeks to Sobriety.* I did the show because I truly thought it would be some revolutionarily fabulous thing, that we could all get together and talk about: the great news that can help everyone suffering from this disease!

The wonderful information available about the biochemical connections to our disease, yeah!

The treatment and help available so we can end cravings, yippee.

The wonderful advances made in the field of biochemistry and alcoholism during the last twenty years . . . what could be better!

You'd think everyone in the audience, alcoholics, would have been thrilled.

Not so fast, Sherlock, 'cause that ain't what happened.

You wouldn't believe the anger, the resentment, the them-against-us position that these people took when it was even suggested that there could be something we hadn't considered. If you are so sure you've got the true answer (eternal life, the truth, the light, the way, or Bill Wilson's 1930s version etched in stone), what are you sooooo afraid of? What harm is there in opening and discussing? What's got you all so uptight?

Here's what has happened over the years.

!!!

You can't talk about AA without talking about Bill Wilson. He's the man (even though there was Dr. Smith, the partner, it's Bill everyone refers to—charismatic, you know!). He started drinking at twenty-two and didn't put the bottle down till it fell out of his hands in one of his many blackouts—panhandling, pawning-everything-he-owned-to pay-for-the-booze episodes.

It was after another "I can't believe that happened" that Bill was admitted to a hospital, where he had what he refers to as his spiritual awakening . . .

"I found myself crying out, 'If there is God, let him show himself. I am ready to do anything.' Suddenly the room lit up with a great white light. All about me there was a wonderful feeling of presence and I thought to myself, 'So this is the God of the preacher.'"

And that was it. The beginning of Alcoholics Anonymous. Bill partnered with Dr. Smith, who after meeting Bill stopped drinking forever, and off they went. In search of other drunks who needed their help.

In 1938 Bill Wilson wrote the Big Book, AA's bible, and what a book it was!

The Big Book is based on Bill and Doc Smith's experience with one hundred white middle-class men and one woman.

The behavior of. The traits of.

arrogant
egocentric
violent
resentful
controlling

That was the assessment of the alcoholic person (middle-class white man) back in 1938. Bill based his program on two things: the traits of the alcoholic man and his own religious experience. Fab. But limited! Fine, but not necessarily applicable today? (Just a thought?) News back then, a great beginning, but the answer? No changes in the last fifty-nine years? No updating? All the research that's been done not included?

Good stuff then, but now?

I went to a seminar recently with the vice president of my company, Lynan, who is in charge of operations, finances, and legal matters—no small job when you're talking me as Captain Stubing.

She graduated years ago with an MBA in whatever you get an MBA in. Smart as hell. Back in the days when there weren't many women in business, she spent years playing the good-old-boys, glass-ceiling business game . . . yeah, yeah, yeah.

We drove together to see this seminar of a very well respected product seller, public speaker, how-to-make-your-business-more-productive guy because I like his stuff and wanted to go see the new guy he'd just appointed top-dog speaker. I'm a public speaker, he's a public speaker, we both do "how to" products, so I'm there.

Halfway through the first few hours (so that would be about an hour in?) my friend and vice president leans over and starts talking about something that was astounding to me and had so very much to do with alcoholism and the current recovery thinking.

She's telling me that one of the reasons why this principle (that's a big clue—I'm not talking skin care, I'm talking business—think, think, think about who it could be) stuff is flying off the shelves is because the people this guy is talking to, upper-middle-class white men in middle-to-upper-management positions, have no principles. This information is news to these boys. They weren't taught these concepts in business school, and they are eating this up like hungry children!

She was amazed. When she went through business school she didn't hear principle-based leadership. (There, I said it. Now if you still don't know who I'm talking about, don't ever do crossword puzzles—not your forte.) She was taught how to get someone to do what you want them to do. Behavioral. How to make them do it.

Now it's all about win-win. Don't be threatened. Surround yourself with people who are as good as, if not better than, you! Nothing early-eighties about that mentality. Enlightenment, encouragement, support, understanding, respect . . . not huge words in business school just a few short years ago. Now it's the rage.

Well, same thing. Yep, same thing when you're talking about the foundation of AA. The focus on humility because there wasn't much of it going on with the first one hundred men, who had to admit that something had them by the nuts? Powerlessness harped on because it may not have been something that they ever considered in their lives before then—why would they? Upper-middle-class and white just about says it all.

We aren't talking about that anymore when you say the word *alcoholic*.
We're talking

women
men
white, black, and every color under the sun
teenagers
young children
sexually abused
every religion out there

Do you really need to harp on powerlessness when you are talking to a woman trying to recover from alcoholism who is living with a husband who beats the hell out of her? I don't know. Moral inventory necessary for all?

That's not what Bill would have wanted. Read about him and you'll find that he was a very cool, very innovative, wonderful man who would have embraced the research of the last thirty-nine years. He would have been hungry for the information that's available and can make all the difference in the world in you and me getting and staying sober!

You're talking about the man who brought upper-middle-class drinking out of the closet. The father of AA was open to opinions and possibilities. This guy looked into psychic phenomena, experimented with LSD, used Ouija boards.

Bill wouldn't ignore years of research. There is no way a person like that would encourage or support the evangelical fervor that is all over the organization he started. I don't think there is a chance in hell that this man would not have been concerned with and tried to understand *why,* and done whatever was necessary to get the help to the millions of alcoholic people who aren't getting helped by AA.

Do you really think a guy like that wouldn't listen to study after study over the last thirty-nine years and make the changes needed to be made??

Of course he'd update. Not only would he include the wonderful biochemical information that's available now for treatment of your disease; he would have been one of the researchers at the head of the team. That's what he was working on when he died. Yep. The biochemical connection to the disease of alcoholism. The vitamin connection. The sugar connection. The white flour connection. The caffeine connection . . . Bill was right there just before he died, of emphysema. (Hello, smoking. Who knew back then? OH, the tobacco industry did but they forgot to tell us). You can bet he would have been interested and so will you . . .

Sober How

!''!

Everything bad that's happened to me has been connected to alcohol—the same cycle has repeated itself over and over again. Maiming myself, losing jobs, motorcycle accidents, three car accidents, losing my wife and my son.

I've lost everything. It's hard to think about the things I've lost, the people I hurt and let down.

It's a cycle I've lived with since I was thirteen—alcoholic drinking.

I've broken it a few times. When I did get sober, I felt irritable, had no attention span, felt grumpy. I didn't know what feeling normal was. I'd get sober and wonder if this is the way it was supposed to feel—having irrational thoughts, craving sugar, not being able to concentrate. It felt worse than thinking about nothing but getting a drink, which is worse than being drunk.

When I finally got introduced to a program for sobriety that gave me nutritional counseling, I got on those vitamins and stopped drinking. It's not only the craving for alcohol that's gone. I can focus. I feel calm, just feel normal. After I started taking the vitamins, I felt better than I had since I was ten years old. I feel healthy, strong—I have a future.

—Mark Powter (Susan's brother)

Those were some of the things my brother told me after he'd begun "nutritional therapy" for alcoholism and was finally staying sober. That's the brother that America is all too familiar with. The brother that went on *Inside Edition* and interviewed with the *Globe,* making the infamous statement, "SHE WAS NEVER TWO HUNDRED AND SIXTY POUNDS."

To be getting the answers now to the questions that everyone who loves Mark had while he was held hostage for twenty years by this monster is one of the greatest feelings of my life. This sounds dramatic, and extreme to anyone who hasn't dealt with the effects of this hateful disease, but all of us who have lived with someone we love being taken by alcoholism understand what it feels like to have the privilege of seeing that person come through this thing. He's back, and I'm so grateful. The bright, interesting, funny, wonderful Mark is back.

|""|

Do you wanna stop drinking and stay stopped? Do you want to *cure alcoholism?* I know, I know, it's a big claim. Believe me, nobody knows that better than me.

You couldn't imagine what a stink this cure-versus-treatment-versus-handle-versus-manage created in discussion after discussion about the marketing and selling of this book . . . Should we—could we—how can I possibly say *cure* when it comes to alcoholism?

The brightest minds in the book business, bickering back and forth about what *cure* REALLY means.

I'm on the other end, in my jammies (always in the jammies when I'm writing all day), listening, getting more and more clear about the need for this book, and thinking about the logic . . .

Let's break down a couple of other diseases, shall we?

You have *heart disease* and a cholesterol level of 310.

You get your cholesterol level down to 150 (proven to be virtual immunity against heart disease, and very possible).

You manage your life and "reverse the disease." You haven't had a heart attack in ten years, you are no longer a heart patient. You have cured, reversed, healed the disease.

Let's talk *cancer* . . .

Some guy just got the diagnosis of prostate cancer.

He did his research, got the facts. Surgery versus internal and external radiation.

He goes down to the clinic.

Gets the radiation.

His PSA level is great.

If it stays that way for a certain period of time, he is free and clear . . .

Breast cancer. Catch it in time.

Treat it.

And be free of it . . . no longer a breast cancer patient.

"I had breast cancer."

"Had heart disease."

"I had prostate cancer."

I've heard it over and over again.

You are addicted to *drugs*.

You get treatment, you haven't done drugs in years.

You have solved the problem, right? Cured your drug addiction?

Smoker . . . all your life?

You stop, it's been five years since you've had a ciggy . . . are you still a smoker?

No.

You are not a heart patient forever.

You are not a cancer patient forever.

You are not a smoker forever . . .

Why are you an alcoholic forever?

Yes, I'm using the word *cure*. Yes, it's the right word . . . no worries, mate, it's not such a big claim (although I fully expect the media to jump on it like flies on . . . but what can you do about that?).

Addicted people can get unaddicted. It is more than possible to repair the internal damage that has been done, and because of the brilliance of this machine that houses our heart and soul—le bodie, with it's unbelievable bounce-back ability—you can treat your disease, cure your disease.

There is one thing all of us, every addict under the sun, has to do before we cure our disease. Before any of the magic of sobriety will ever be a part of our lives, one quick thing we need to do . . .

YOU GOTTA GIVE IT UP . . . (Are you thinking of

throwing the book against the wall? Don't blame you, but read on, give it a second . . . don't judge a book by its content right now.)

If you are going to get sober and stay that way, you are going to have to give it up.

Come out with your hands high in the air.

Up against the wall.

Put the weapon down and get on the ground . . .

Drinking has got you by the throat and throttles you every time you do it. You, my friend, like me and all the other millions of alcoholics, will never, ever win when you step into the ring with Muhammad—yes, The Man—Ali. And that's exactly what you are doing every time you put the bottle to your lips. Fighting the world champion of all time, without the class . . .

Male, female, young, old, color, religion, background —no difference. Not one of us has a chance against Ali. Put the gloves down and walk the hell out of the gym. Retire, surrender. It's over.

That's what you have to know. That's what you have to surrender to, understand without a doubt before you can get and stay sober. You ain't never gonna win against this thing!

Think of it this way, a couple of times a week someone suggests you go down to your local gym (yeah, like the Rocky neighborhood gym is a reality for any of us!) and fight. One on one. You and the strongest person on the planet. Mr. World Champion . . . ???

Get yourself a robe. (Very shiny, very red usually works well in the boxer/wrestler world.) Make sure you've got yourself someone to go down with you to rub your shoulders, shove some water in your mouth, to be there to slap you in the face a couple of times in between each round . . . very boxing.

How many rounds in this sport—ten, fifteen, or something? Who knows, who cares? 'Cause you ain't gonna last ten seconds, let alone ten rounds, of nothing with Ali!

Give it up, 'cause you ain't gonna win, ever!

Hold the flag up, walk out with your hands high in the air, up against the wall, motherfucker, 'cause it's over . . . it's time to surrender. And that is the first step in *sober how* . . .

Fighting

A funny thing happened to me in the therapist's office one day. By watching someone fight, I finally began to understand the word *surrender*.

I asked Rusty to come to Mark's office (my therapist, not the brother) with me because I needed someone to hear what I already knew, and as you have probably figured out by now, I was asking Rusty to do a lot of Sober 101 with me at this stage of the game. I needed to tell the truth about the pain I'd been in for so long. Sometimes, like when you're so scared you can't function, you just have to include someone, trust someone enough, and speak it.

Yeah, fine, a good, healthy, functional thing to do, very, very mentally healthy of me, wouldn't you say? It only took an absolutely disastrous four months of fighting and NOT winning (my last four months of drinking) and years of drinking before that to get me there, so let's not go nuts on *Maturity and Healing,* by Susan Powter . . . But hey, I was there. I was ready to speak the truth and tell someone what was going on, and I did.

Mark the therapist (oh, so very Hollywood) and I explained to Rusty what being alcoholic means—the power of the addiction that I was living with / dying from. The total destruction that this disease thrives on. The suffering and the pain that's created by the disease of alcoholism. And we explained that someone Rusty loves very, very much—me—was sick and needed help.

I can honestly tell you, looking back over the course of the last twenty years at birth, death, loss, love, divorce, pain, revelations, gut-wrenching work of all kinds, that nothing I had done before this moment had ever felt more difficult, more painful, and seemed more hopelessly impossible to achieve than going from addicted to unaddicted . . . drinking to sober.

To speak the words *I am alcoholic.* To tell the truth about this disease . . .

That it was controlling my life.

That it was going to ruin everything in my life.

That it was going to kill me.

And that I was desperately afraid I couldn't stop . . .

To be actually taking part in telling someone, helping someone understand, the thing I'd known and had hidden from and was so very afraid of for so long was not fun, not fun, not fun.

Saying the words *I am alcoholic and I am going to stop drinking forever* . . .

Feeling the feelings that I'd been drowning in alcohol for sooo long was hateful, hateful, hateful.

• • •

As soon as Rusty heard what had been going on and what it all meant, she started to fight. It's one of the things that I love the most about Rusty. When she loves, she loves big. When she believes, she believes big. When she's committed, she's totally committed. And when she fights, she fights with everything she's got, and that's exactly what she did.

"We're gonna BEAT this thing, Sus . . .

"It's OK. You just are never, ever, ever gonna drink again, we'll MAKE SURE of it.

"We'll learn everything there is to learn about it, and we'll CONQUER it."

Finally, when I was watching someone else fight for me, I saw it.

"Rusty, don't you understand what I'm the most afraid of . . . ?

"I can't fight this thing.

"It's the only thing in my life that I've never been able to figure a way out of by myself. I've been trying. It's not working. It got me. It's in me and I don't know how to get it out . . . I can't fight it."

That's what I'd been trying to do in my last few months of drinking. Fight it—fight it with all my might—and I was getting the everliving hell beaten out of me! You see, I was still under the impression that I could fight Ali. There was still something in me that hung on to the belief that there was some way, some strategy, something that meant enough to me that I would figure out a way to "have only one."

I tried and tried and it always ended the same way . . . beaten.

That's what I mean when I say you gotta give up.

Give up believing that you can have just one.

Give up pretending that this thing hasn't gotten out of hand.

Stop justifying why it always seems to end up badly.

Stop minimizing it.

Stop hiding from it.

Stop lying about it.

Just give up, you, me, right here and now . . . understand, believe, receive one thing. You ain't never gonna win. Not if you keep drinking.

There is a way to control alcoholism, and I've found it. Abstinence. That's not a problem, and what you have in your hands is going to make it very, very clear how you can do that for the rest of your life.

But what I'm asking you to do now, what is necessary —the beginning, the foundation of the whole thing, and what I and millions of other recovered addicts had to do first is . . .

You gotta know that you can never, ever control, fight, win if you are drinking. You have to understand that no amount of fighting to make it normal is ever going to make a difference. You will never be able to do it responsibly. To just have a cocktail. To unwind a bit.

That's never gonna happen.

There is no fighting this thing. There is no way. So run from the bully.

Every time you get in the ring with the bottle, you will be beaten.

Admit what you've seen happening in your life every time you drink. You are getting the hell beat out of you. Just admit that. Nothing more, just that!

I was never, ever, ever, ever, ever going to win. It was never gonna happen. The beatings were getting worse and worse.

My last few months of fighting left me broken, battered, bruised, drained, so frightened, and feeling completely out of control in my own life.

Everything seemed fine on the surface. I was doing videos and audios, developing products, teaching classes, had a lovely home, was mothering my sons, running my life in complete control, till I touched a drop of alcohol.

That's my truth.

Then, faster than I could ever have imagined, worse than I ever wanted to know from . . . I turned into a slobbering, staggering, stupid idiot. Every damn time. It never failed.

I was watching the progression of my disease as if it was happening to someone else . . .

From three or four beers to twenty-six???

Drinking in the middle of the day? Absolutely! Before I knew it, it was wine at lunch.

Get-together with friends, drinking—from three times a week to every other day . . . It was happening without me even noticing till there wasn't a day that went by when I wasn't recovering from a hangover . . .

First thing in the morning—cognac because I had a sore throat? It happened.

But the truth was—cognac because my hands were

shaking from the night before and I wanted to calm down a bit.

The lies, the pain, the building of a fatal progressive disease. It's gonna happen as long as you keep drinking. No amount of fighting and determination I had or you have can stop this thing as long as we keep drinking.

When I say give it up, I'm not talking alcohol. You'll know how to stop and stay stopped once you understand the disease you have and how to treat it. I'm talking about giving up the belief that you can find a way to manage your drinking.

Here's where Ali comes in, figuratively, not literally (could you imagine?). I can't fight Ali, no matter how long I train, no matter what I do. There are some things in this life you just can't do . . . and fighting him and winning would be one of them. And the same applies to drinking. Truth. I knew it and so do you. Surrender to that! Right now, for the second it takes, just surrender to that.

Surrender

Surrender.

Hate the word! Couldn't hate a word more than *surrender,* if you want to know the whole truth and nothing but the truth. As a woman who struggles every day with the issues of independence, financial, emotional . . . in business, as a girlfriend, friend, mother. Surrender—no chance!

My God, I've spent the last couple of years (and don't even ask about the struggle during the last thirteen years, since the kids were born; since I got fat, then fit; since I went through two divorces—reread this line, put yourself in my shoes, and see if you don't feel like the biggest loser in town for a second) struggling for the right to be independent.

Any minority understands that no matter what the pretty picture being painted is, the truth of the matter is that we are miles away from equality. So count me in forever in the walk toward freedom and equality for women! Nothing is gonna sway me from this.

Here I sit in my life, cemented in my commitment toward independence . . . couldn't love much more than I do having the independence that I have in my life. You won't see me giving it up for anybody or anything!

Hey, I know from my own "independent" life experience that if you want a loving relationship with someone, anyone—kids, boyfriends, girlfriends, coworkers, whomever—it's independence first so that you can be a whole person in a healthy interdependent relationship. That's it. That's the relationship law and it just can't happen without independence.

Know that. Live that. Fine.

Come on, you're talking to a woman (writer's creative privilege) convinced beyond a shadow of a doubt that having my own money, being financially, emotionally, and spiritually independent, is the only way on earth to come to all the wonderful interdependent relationships that I/you/we all need to be healthy, balanced human beings.

Independence, strength, courage, conviction are big words in the Powter household.

• • •

I have fought like hell to get fit, strong, and get my physical independence back, and it worked. I've been swimming upstream in business for the last five years, sweating blood to do it right—an ounce of integrity, boys, please! —and it's working.

Fought the biggest litigation of my life, the only one I'd ever fought up until then. Now, when it comes to being sued, my motto is—*Take a ticket and stand in line.*

I fought long and hard, pouring out the cash to buy back my independence from a schmuck. I've been fighting against the big boys who run the whole show—the TV show, the radio show, the video show . . . all the shows.

Fight, team, fight, our company motto . . . (All ex-cheerleaders, including me, I might add—I was on the team for a while, then they asked me to leave for kissing M.M., but they didn't ask M.M. to leave the basketball team. I had to resign as cheerleader, but he could still play on the team??? What did I kiss—a wall, or Matthew? Completely different subject, I'm aware, but just had to make the statement.)

Go, fabulous women in my company, Go . . . Don't ever give up. Keep fighting, keep moving forward, keep producing quality.

Quit anything? Over my dead body. They'll have to kill me . . . That's the spirit in most win-win situations in our lives, right?

That's how I came face-to-face with the diet industry, the AMA, the TV boys who want to pigeonhole women and take them back to *Father Knows Best* days . . . Well, he doesn't . . .

Slash, slash, slash my way through the corporate, putrid jungle . . .

Stand up and fight when the PTA is trying to implement programs that discriminate against children who learn differently. No more molding into standard, antiquated learning . . .

Boot the coach on the baseball team who screams at the kids and calls them idiots . . .

Fight him, fight it, work, stand up, move forward, take the bull by the horns . . . except, of course, if it's running through the town square in Spain, 'cause I've seen that video of the person who got gouged through the thigh . . . Hello. Bull horn through the thigh. Just spend a second and think about that!

So there I sat, having worked hard, comfortable in my place, at peace with what I know to be true. Happy and clear about my fight for independence, growth, and understanding, yes, yes, yes . . . And I find out that I have a disease that could easily ruin everything I've worked for . . . and the beginning of the healing is in completely and absolutely understanding, embracing, and living the word *surrender!!!*

Excuse me. Pick another word, maybe, but I ain't surrendering to you, Mama, because I don't surrender. There, that's it. I'll just find another way. Screw *surrender* . . .

My response??? Hateful at best . . .

ABSOLUTELY NOT. No chance in hell is that ever gonna happen. When I heard the word *surrender* I got what the ex-addict I was talking to (otherwise known as my therapist) called a *visceral response*. My first question was, "What in the hell does *visceral* mean?" Answer: a physical response, to my core, angry, nauseous—which was exactly what I was having at his suggestion of surrendering to anything, anybody, any, any, any surrender of any kind . . . No! Won't do it.

Anger?

Resentment . . .

Resistance . . .

My throat started to close—that would be the visceral response . . . I'm telling you the truth when I tell you that I couldn't breathe . . . This is not a good thing when your calling card is oxygen!

My thoughts about getting sober at that time were, *Fight, team, fight. Surrender, my butt. It's not going to beat me. I'll do everything I have to do to kill this monster. I'm here to do battle and I'll fight till it's over, but don't ever mention the* word surrender *to me again because you can bet that I'm gonna find a way to beat this thing.* And that's exactly what I tried to do for four months. I tried to fight alcoholism. And fight I did.

All the way to the gutter . . .

The first time I absolutely quit drinking? I did. Eight days of fighting the urge to quit drinking. Eight days of believing that I could beat this thing. Days of really believing that I knew how to not drink anymore. That my level of commitment and conviction was enough. That no matter what, I wasn't picking up the bottle.

Check out the words I was using. *Beat this thing . . . Fighting . . .* I'd *find a way*—and??? *Surrender* nowhere in sight. And that thinking? Led me right into my beyond-the-shadow-of-hell crawl to the gutter, the worst four months of my life, all of the forementioned . . . and it had everything in the world to do with surrendering versus fighting.

● ● ●

You see, my first crash-and-burn with drinking was on Valentine's Day, otherwise known as Rusty's birthday, otherwise known as the-most-horrible-party-in-the-world-that-to-this-day-I-think-about-and-get-a-chill-up-my-spine . . . visceral gal that I am.

I'll nutshell this because that's all that's needed. As usual, the way it "happened" is as embarrassingly typical and textbook as you get . . . and as always, it started as no big deal.

I'm throwing a birthday party for a dear friend the evening of. I leave the business meeting late afternoon—long day, long week—and thought to myself as I was driving up the street on the way to the store to pick up little Valentine's gifts for my children . . . i.e., the letter. Just before I go home and get ready for the party . . . I think, *Boy, I'd like a drink.* Nothing more, nothing less.

Just that thought, *Wouldn't it be nice to have a drink?* Innocent enough, normal enough. Who doesn't think that once in a while after a long, hard day?

So I stopped at the store to get that drink.

That night I ended up so drunk I couldn't stand, couldn't speak, couldn't enjoy or remember a lot of the party that I was throwing for someone I love very dearly. I had my first blackout that night. (Couldn't believe it. Me . . . blacking out, progression, progression—just another "Can't believe that happened to ME" that happens in the destructive path of this disease.)

I made a complete fool of myself. I was so sick the next morning I literally couldn't get out of bed. I lied to my children about why I couldn't take them to school, tried desperately to start my day, and couldn't because I was vomiting so much . . . and for the first time in my life,

I called someone (Rusty) and asked her to come over and help me. The scraping off the bathroom floor? This was it. Rusty scraping me off to the alcohol recovery therapist, where I said the words *I am alcoholic* for the first time.

Hey, I went to therapy that next day and I said the words *I am an alcoholic.* Nobody in the world could have been more committed to quitting drinking than I was at that moment in my life. No more pain and misery. I couldn't do it anymore. I knew that after this "incident," and having already spoken the words *I'm alcoholic,* sharing the pain and fear with someone, in therapy for alcoholism . . . come on. I was doing it. Doing what it took, working on sober, being big about the whole thing, suffering, and confessing (very Catholic), and I did stop drinking. COMPLETELY AND ABSOLUTELY FOR EIGHT DAYS. Then I drank myself into the toilet for four months.

And let me be the first to tell you (what you probably already know): if I thought the morning after that party was bad . . . never in my wildest imagination (and believe me, I've got a wild one) could I have conjured up anything like what was about to happen to me in the progression of this disease. I could no more have foreseen the next four months than fly in the air!

I was busy, busy, busy. Busy fighting the disease. Working hard to beat this thing that had a hold on my life.

Getting in the ring with the world champion and trying to beat it. Remember, don't mention the word *surrender* to me.

I didn't want to have anything to do with it, and I didn't, because I was convinced that I could beat this beast!

• • •

Some folks would tell me that I was in denial because I couldn't immediately surrender.

All because I wasn't willing to hang my brain on the coatrack and just go along every time I heard the word *surrender* didn't mean that I was in denial. I wasn't. I knew I was an alcoholic and had known for a long time, but the word *surrender* didn't make any sense to me, so I didn't do it.

ı⁣ıⁱ⁣ı⁣ı

Surrender

Maybe this will make sense to you.

Surrender. The new version.

You may feel, as I did, that the word *surrender* is the dumbest word under the sun and that it should be banned from the human language. You may be convinced, as I was, that there isn't a stupider (and she writes for a living, folks) word around. And it is, until you understand it.

And there is nothing wrong with needing to understand it.

There is nothing wrong with getting a second opinion. Don't know any other disease where a second opinion isn't encouraged and supported. As a matter of fact, you are a fool if you don't get one these days—except, of course, with our disease??? The disease of alcoholism.

Of course you should understand it. Why wouldn't you want something to make sense to you before you invest your heart and soul in it? (One of the reasons I don't do well in organized religion is because I need to understand the logic, get the facts, ask the questions I need to ask . . . No can do. Kicked out of church every time . . .)

The way I figured it then and the way I figure it now—
that there isn't any other disease I can think of that anyone
with a brain in their head wouldn't tell you to investigate
. . . ask questions, fully understand, take responsibility,
and do as much as you can to participate in your healing.
So that's exactly what we are going to do, and it begins
with understanding what surrendering means and how to
apply it to your non-drinking life.

Don't surrender because you think you are a powerless
piece of junk. You aren't.
    Don't give in.
    Don't give up.
    Here's what I've learned about surrender:

a. You absolutely have the right to, and should,
    understand what surrendering to your disease
    means in order to apply it to your life.

b. You are going to apply it frequently in sobriety.

    and

c. You have to do it in order to stay stopped drink-
    ing. (Not within seconds or perfectly or in blind
    faith, but you gotta do it.)

Surrender to this . . .

You have a progressive fatal disease.

Your body does not process alcohol the same way
    a nonalcoholic body does. Surrender to that.

You are one of the 10 percent of the population who are addicted to alcohol. Surrender to that.

You have tried to quit and fail every time. Surrender to that.

Sobriety is going to take work, education, commitment, practice, truth, and guts. Surrender to that. You are willing to do it because you want to be well, you want to be sober, and you want your life back. Surrender to that.

You want to get sober and stay that way, surrender to the truth about how well you fight against this thing? Get real honest about the beatings.

There isn't a problem understanding the beatings the next day, when you are in the middle of one of those blinding-headaches, sweaty-palms, horribly-sick-stomach mornings after. You're real clear about the beating when you are battered and bruised.

There is no question that you are not the winner when you are trying desperately to pull yourself together to get the kids to school, get to the meeting, or just get the hell out of bed . . . You ain't drinking no more, just like you're not having a baby ever again at six or seven centimeters dilated—but a couple of days later it's amazing how fast the memory of the worst beating of your life disappears. It's astounding how fast this thing has us convinced that it wasn't really that bad.

Surrender to how bad it really is.

My God, I didn't want to fall in front of my friend Lisa, but I did.

I had to surrender to that.

Never in my life did I want to be too drunk to talk to the baby-sitter when I got home, but I was.

Surrender to that one!

It's hard to face the nights I drove home so drunk I couldn't see straight and the danger that my drinking put me and everyone else who was on the road those nights in . . . Surrender!

I WASN'T GOING TO WIN. That's all I had to surrender to. I knew that.

It's not important right now to know how, you are ever gonna not drink.

It doesn't matter how broken your faith is when it comes to knowing you will not drink.

You don't have to be able to think beyond this minute. Just know this:

As long as you continue to drink, you are practicing the philosophy you want to change.

And surrender.

Don't surrender out of weakness. Surrender in strength, the strength of being able to live in the truth, the courage to be honest with yourself about your drinking. It has nothing to do with you being a big weenie. Be honest about the fact that this alcohol beats the hell out of you every time it gets into your system . . . You know it's true. Have a look at the last few months. Tell me it ain't so.

How about giving up what doesn't work and trying something that does—surrendering to the truth and not trying to beat the unbeatable?

Take responsibility for the victim here—you. Protect him/her, take care of him/her, give yourself shelter, love, understanding, a place to heal and get better, and learn,

learn, learn about your disease. Find out everything there is to know about this progressive, fatal disease that you were born with, alcoholism, and get on with solving the problem.

!!!

I've got a question for you. How many times has this happened? . . .

The earth is flat. That's it, no other way of thinking possible. Everyone in the world is convinced. Until somebody says, "Sorry, folks, it's round."

Let's go back just a bit. October 1492. Queen Isabella wanted this cocky navigator named Christopher to go to China for trade.

She gives him the old *Pinta, Niña,* and *Santa Maria* and says, "Bring me back some ramen, babe."

Chris, the only man on the planet who was convinced that the world was round, figured he'd test his little theory and go west, AROUND to his destination.

Funny thing happened on the way to pick up the take-out . . . he bumped into a couple of islands (filled with casinos that Donald Trump owned) called the Bahamas.

You'd think that would be enough for this young navigator, but being the navigator he was, he continued.

Between 1492 and 1502 the guy made four trips. The first couple he hung in Donald's part of the world, did the Bahamas thing for a while. Venturing out on the last two trips, almost tripping over the island of Martinique, that French-speaking, sexy little island that you go to just after the wedding, he's sailing by, he's grooving, and he bumps into a larger chunk of land . . . South America, the land filled with so many countries you can hardly keep track.

Central America, to this day a place you mention any-where, anytime, just throw it out, and you'll instantly see that nobody knows anything about it . . . Give it a try at your next party. Go ahead, you'll have nothing better to do, YOU WON'T BE DRINKING. (A little may-have-been-a-tad-distasteful-but-you-gotta-admit-it's-funny sober joke.) Back to Christopher Columbus . . .

He's going, he's sailing, he's been around and around and finally . . . the big one, the ultimate find.

America.

Stumbled upon it, never really knowing what hit him, according to rumor. (And what kind of navigator was he?) He's thinking he's still in Asia, looking everywhere for China. (There's an even bigger rumor floating—navigating pun—around, that he never really discovered America. A whole other story, but let's say, for the sake of being able to get back to the subject at hand—drinking too much—that he did.)

Turns out that some 504 years later this little naviga-tional mess is an important piece of the puzzle and a great help to people who are dealing with the disease of alcoholism.

Columbus and alcoholism connected???

Sure it is.

The flat-world believers don't even want to know from anyone saying that the world is round. The flat-worlders aren't interested in the decades of research that has proven over and over again that the reason you drink has very little to do with willpower, morality, weakness of will. None of those things have anything on earth (a round earth, I might add) to do with why you and I are alcoholic.

• • •

Let's get down to the facts so you can get on with the solution and on with your life.

We are going to do two things at once:

Understand and get the truth, about how alcohol affects you—the bio-chemical *nutritional* stuff.

And simultaneously, smash the myths, expose the reasons why the lies continue to be funded and encouraged, and how it interferes with your sobriety cover—the *behavioral* junk.

These two things work together in helping you stay stopped, and here's how.

The nutritional support that has so very much to do with your sick, craving, poisoned body and mind and the treatment for our disease.

And cleaning up the behavioral cobwebs? If you want the best tool in your daily building and in working your sobriety, it's in understanding what's going on—why, how, and being a part of changing the thinking that has kept recovery from millions of people.

If you want to live your sobriety in reality and not in misinformation and lies, if you want to stay rational rather than irrational, understand what is going on during your first couple of months of sobriety, and know best how to deal with it so that you can maintain the life that we've tried to get a thousand times before—a sober life—then I'm assuming that you, like me, will find the information about what's going on inside your body with your disease helpful in alleviating some of the mystery, the fear and the shame that may have been all over you and this drinking problem you've been having.

Planting something tangible and understandable, making sense of it all, and figuring out the solution seems the way to go, don't you think?

Because the truth of your drinking matter is:

"It is no more logical to blame the alcoholic for altered behavior than to demand accountability from someone with Alzheimer's disease."

OK, let's start there! We are off, off to one hell of a beginning.

HOW IN THE HELL COULD ANYONE MAKE THAT STATEMENT OR RESPONSIBLY PRINT IT IN A BOOK!!!

Because we are going to be talking about nutrition and behavior together . . . and we can't talk about either one without talking *poison*. You and me being poisoned.

I don't know about you, but the first thing I think of when I think of poison is the little old ladies with arsenic and old lace and with all the dead bodies in the basement. Dead. Poison.

Really sick.

Skull-and-bones poisoning, is exactly what's been happening to us.

Every time you drink, you are poisoning yourself. Six major organs—your brain, heart, liver, pancreas, lungs, and kidneys—are being poisoned. And the one that's affected most by alcohol, your brain. The behavioral center of it all!

The control tower is being poisoned? What do you

think is gonna happen to incoming flights, landings, and takeoffs? Behavior not affected? I don't think so. Hand in hand, just like I told ya.

And it all apparently starts with the liver.

Yeah, yeah . . . cirrhosis jokes left, right, and center for the old alky. But beyond the jokes the truth is: our disease and the liver are very much connected in the building of our alcoholism way before cirrhosis ever becomes a reality.

Here's how our bodies drink.

We take a sip of alcohol and our liver starts to break it down into AS-A-TOL-DA-HYDE. It's officially spelled *acetaldehyde,* but I'll be breaking it down phonetically every time I type it because I can't pronounce it to save my life, and I figure I may as well take this opportunity to learn the word—under the guise that I will be helping you pronounce it. So, class, here's the word.

AS-A-TOL-DA-HYDE.

As-a-tol-da-hyde is the deadly poisonous chemical that alcohol turns into in the human liver. Everyone's liver. As-a-tol-da-hyde equals poison. As-a-tol-da-hyde isn't a problem for most bodies, because *most bodies* can take, drink the alcohol, turn it into as-a-tol-da-hyde, and quickly turn it into acetate (which is the next step in the elimination of this poison from the human body). Then *most bodies* brilliantly and efficiently eliminate it through the skin, the breath, and urine . . . poison in, poison out, quickly and efficiently. Again, hats off to this body of ours!

That's how it works in *their* bodies (the ones who really leave after one cocktail). Ours, on the other hand, do one step of the normal process (breaking alcohol into as-a-tol-da-hyde) too fast, and the other step (turning it into acetate to be eliminated from the body) too slowly, creating such problems, don't ask!

Seems that my/our as-a-tol-da-hyde levels produced in the old liver are different than in the infuriating person that can actually order a glass of wine, have a few sips, and leave what they don't want . . . that obnoxious nonalcoholic.

"Research shows the same amount of alcohol produced very different blood acetaldehyde levels in alcoholics and nonalcoholics."

And guess where that abnormal level is produced. In the liver. Yep, the home that houses the cirrhosis in the years to come.

"Abnormal Metabolism—Acetaldehyde, the intermediate byproduct of alcohol metabolism, appears to be one of the major villains in the onset of alcoholic drinking . . . and it begins in the liver."

Abnormal metabolism of alcoholism??? My liver cannot do what yours can?

Sir, you have insulted me. I challenge you to a duel . . .

But it's true.

And our abnormal metabolism? It's a liver that's just not doing it right. So what is the first thing you think? Our liver does it too slow? Not efficiently enough? Nope, not at all. Quite the opposite. Alcoholics break this stuff down into as-a-tol-da-hyde way too FAST.

Faster than the average Joe or Josephine, who can drink just a couple and break it down properly. Not us. We've got loads of this poison breaking down too fast in our liver (and we keep drinking), and it builds up. See potential for problems here?

> **"This foul-up in processing allows the poisonous byproduct of alcohol, acetaldehyde, to build up in the cell causing a great deal of damage."**

> **"The liver mitochondria [and I'll explain later what those little pods are] are abnormal and unable to change acetaldehyde into acetate at as great a rate as in non-alcoholics."**

This is the beginning of understanding what physically happens in our bodies that doesn't happen in nonalcoholics' bodies.

You've got to understand the physiological makeup of our disease.

Which helps you understand why we drink.

Why you have trouble not drinking.

How your behavior is affected by your drinking.

How none of it has anything to do with your character.

And how it has everything to do with your liver breaking alcohol down into as-a-tol-da-hyde too fast and doing the second step of the process too slow.

Marc Schuckit, psychiatrist and researcher at the University of California, took the liver breakdown one step further and found that "the breakdown of acetaldehyde in acetate, the second step in alcohol metabolism, is performed at half the rate of normal, non-alcoholic metabolism."

Oh no, sound the alarms. Think about this.

We've got this stuff building up because our livers break it down fast, fast, fast, and the other half of the process, of getting this stuff out of your body (converting as-a-tol-da-hyde into acetate), is taking its everloving time. Half the rate of the average Josephine.

Just think about what this could possibly mean. Poison (which is alcohol—double jeopardy) is in everybody's body, because everybody has a drink.

That poison is breaking down faster in our bodies.

And being turned into the eliminating acetate slower than you could imagine. What do you think is happening? We are being poisoned.

It escapes . . .

Sound the alarms, and this time—BRING OUT THE DOGS, because you and I have as-a-tol-da-hyde escaping through our livers and going . . . where???

Straight to our brain. Poison in the brain. Are you beginning to understand the poison and behavior connection?

Brain poisoning—that's always a good thing?

The as-a-tol-da-hyde is running through your blood, busting the blood-brain barrier, and whammo! The escapee kicks in the door of the house (your brain) and holds you hostage (just what you'd expect from an escapee worth his salt), affecting your behavior (more than you could ever imagine), taking control of how you act, how much you need alcohol (addiction is a brain disease), affects your decision making (getting in that car after your brain has been poisoned has nothing to do with good decision making or how responsible you are). You have been poisoned. You are being held hostage. Your brain is under siege . . . But our terrorist situation is different than most.

We are not feeling panic-stricken, fearing-for-our-lives feelings that I'm sure the hostages at the Olympic Village felt. Nope, not at all. That's not what your poisoned brain, the organ that has been taken hostage, is feeling.

You don't have warning signs of panic.

You don't know anything is wrong.

What you are feeling as your brain is being taken hostage is . . .

Complete euphoria!!!

Wrapped in heaven. That's what your poisoned, alcoholic brain is.

Yes, my friends, this as-a-tol-da-hyde has the ability to produce the most amazing effect on your brain. You are in complete and absolute heaven.

A captive in heaven.

Our, the alcoholics', brain's response to as-a-tol-da-hyde is different from the average Joe and Josephine's. Another physiological connection between you, your disease, your behavior, and your sobriety.

After just a couple of drinks, they (the average Joe and Josephine, or the obnoxious nonalcoholic) get tired.

We . . . get heavenly—not in our deeds and actions (we get stupid in those)—euphoric, higher than high, feeling better than they could ever feel . . .

They start to feel sick and dizzy after three or four drinks.

We get a ton of energy.

They get nauseous.

We are ready to go . . . we are just starting!

They get ready for bed. We get ready to party.

They get sick after three shots of whiskey, can you believe it?

That's because the as-a-tol-da-hyde in our brains starts its magic, mixing with other neurotransmitters, and causes the opiate sensation of all time . . . THAT KICK!

It's FANTASTIC when you feel it.

Everything is SOOO MUCH FUN WHEN I'M DRUNK.

I am having SUCH A GOOD TIME.

I love everyone in the room MORE THAN I EVER DREAMED POSSIBLE.

This is beyond question THE BEST PARTY I'VE EVER BEEN TO.

NOTHING COULD BE MORE FUN THAN THIS . . . Whatever it is, it's more fun a couple of beers later. With an opiated brain and loads of as-a-tol-da-hyde floating all over the place, I'm there. Tracy Chapman is right. Heaven is here on earth . . .

Opiate, as in *euphoria*.

Opiate, as in *den*.

Opiate, as in the best feeling you've ever felt. The non-alcoholics don't get that. They can never feel as good as you and I feel when we drink, and . . . they also don't get another thing that comes with opiates . . .

Addicted . . . Opiate, as in *addicted*.

• • •

Why do you think you are having trouble stopping drinking? You are addicted to a drug. The addiction is taking place, quite literally, in our heads.

An opiated head.

Our drinking is addictive. Joe and Josephine's will never be. They can never "become" alcoholic. I always was. You and I will always have the biochemistry that processes alcohol in a way that poisons and addicts.

By the time this stuff hits our brains we may as well be in an opium den, sucking on one of those long water pipes. You want stories of addiction, get a good opium-den story. These boys were totaled by this stuff. It controlled their lives? Completely.

Well, a couple of drinks in, and that's what your brain has become . . .

Our addiction to alcohol is *not psychological* (as some flat-worlders would have you believe—no, no, no, not true at all). You didn't become an alcoholic; you were born with the chemistry to be one. It's *physiological*.

"Like all chronic illnesses, alcoholism begins in a hidden stage when the victim is unaware that anything unusual is going on inside him."

There are stages to walking into this opium den, a couple of different doors you have to pass through before you get to the point where you feel you can never get out . . .

Stage one is the most silent, most confusing, the most

contradictory stage of your disease. Because at this point your drinking is no different from that of all the other frat boys and sorority girls (like I was ever a sorority gal . . . a first stage drinker, absolutely—sorority anything, never). Everyone is drinking, and so are you. Not a problem. You already know that not only can you drink like everyone else, you can do it just a bit better. Always the one who can handle it best, that's you.

No doubt you could drink with the best of them, couldn't you?

I could.

Hold your own? Not a problem! Better than hold your own.

Nothing affected you like it affected them. You didn't get as stupid, you never got as drunk . . . just had a great time and led the pack when it came to a great night out . . .

A lamp shade on the head here or there, but basically not a problem. You were always just a "normal" human being, paying the bills, being responsible, and once in a while having a "good" time. Why would you ever, for a second, give any thought to drinking too much? That would mean that there was a problem, and at this point, there wasn't. Being able to handle alcohol better than most didn't indicate to me that there was a problem; it meant I did it better than them. They had the problem, getting sloppy drunk after just four or five drinks . . . I had the solution. Handle it better, like me!

You drink better than most—I drank better than most—in the beginning. It's loads of fun, and why on earth would you consider giving it up?

You wouldn't. I didn't, because it wasn't a problem at all . . .

"The alcoholic in the early stage of his [their] disease experiences undetectable changes in his [their] cells, changes that will eventually cause his [their] body to adapt to alcohol. The cells are actually adjusting themselves to the presence of alcohol and becoming more efficient at using it as an energy source."

"The early alcoholic does not appear to suffer in any way from drinking. He [they] usually feels happy and carefree when he [they] drinks."

"During this stage alcohol works certain changes in the cells, laying down the groundwork for the massive damage that occurs later. Despite these cellular changes, the alcoholic does not yet act like an alcoholic."

Just like heart disease, you don't know anything right now. You feel great. They feel great. Who knew so much cholesterol was building up?

Who knew the artery was as rotted as it is?

Who knew 90 percent occluded . . . ?

If you were to go to your doctor during the first stages of your disease, not a damn thing would be wrong with you, but what's going on inside of your body is devasta-ting. My cells were adjusting themselves to alcohol.

Who knew?

Those cells of mine were becoming more and more efficient at using alcohol as an energy supply (and supply energy it did, you know that).

Here's where the mitochondria come in. Sounds like a bad horror movie, doesn't it? And in a way it is.

Because the happening place during this "Who's to know something is wrong with you?" stage of your disease is the liver. Your mitochondria are screwed up. Yep, those tiny little podlike things inside each cell that have the job of releasing energy from food are not normal in alcoholics. You and I have visibly distorted mitochondria, can you believe it? You'd think that having stretchy, enlarged mito-chondria would be a problem, and it is eventually, but in the beginning stage of our disease it's a benefit (to our drinking, that is) because "with these changes in cell struc-ture, the liver is able to process alcohol more efficiently and the alcoholic is able to drink increasingly large amounts of alcohol and still function normally."

THAT'S WHY WE CAN DRINK MORE. NOT BE-CAUSE WE HAVE LESS ABILITY TO HANDLE OURSELVES AT A PARTY OR DON'T LOVE WHAT-EVER ENOUGH, BUT BECAUSE OUR MITO-CHONDRIA ARE SCREWED, THAT'S WHY.

See what's happening? The connection is only just be-ginning to be made, but what a connection it is.

Physiological goings-on in our bodies like you've never thought about. Your liver, my liver, your as-a-tol-da-hyde, your acetate, the breakdown that's too fast, and the one that's too slow. Addiction happening without you and me even knowing what's going on in the noggin! And how about those enlarged mitochondria? Again, who knew!

Beginning to see the biochemical–behavioral characteristics–physical combo going on? See how it all works together to explain the disease that 22 million people suffer from? Well, if you're not seeing the link yet, you will, because the information that's right around the corner will cement even the most skeptical into including the need for healing and treating the physical damage that alcohol does to the human body.

〈!!!〉

Did you know that alcohol is one of the richest foods known to man? Can you believe that?

It's also a very, very efficient source of energy. That, you and I know—but here's something I bet you didn't know . . .

Calorie for calorie, every ounce of alcohol is equivalent to

fourteen spears of asparagus
twelve almonds
one orange
a couple of slices of whole-grain bread
two tomatoes

This stuff is amazing. It's got calories, it's a food, it gives you energy, but . . . it's a food with only calories, nothing else.

This stuff, nutritionally, isn't worth anything. Zip. And when you are talking about a food (that we are drinking lots of) with no nutritional value at all, we are looking at a couple of major problems.

Highly caloric, and lots of it. Problem.

No nutritional value, and lots of it. Problem.

Two obvious problems. You're eating stuff that has a lot of calories and it's not doing you a bit of good.

You figure out what that means, because I'm onto the most amazing thing! Something nobody would ever think is happening in the American suburbs today, something that ties this physiological-and-behavioral discussion together like nothing else . . .

Malnutrition. You and I are malnourished.

We can't talk about alcoholism without talking about malnutrition. Chronic malnutrition.

Millions of women in this country have lived with malnutrition (anyone who's ever been on a diet for more than a couple of months), sucking down the powders, shakes, formulas, cider vinegar, grapefruit only, living on the candy bar things. . . . the dieting, the starvation and deprivation, that is normal in our world. (Not only do we volunteer for starvation, we pay thousands and thousands of dollars for someone in a white lab coat to starve us . . . Go figure!) This is one kind of malnutrition, the socially acceptable kind. It is a malnutrition that is encouraged, supported, well, well advertised, and oh-so-beautifully packaged (by another charming industry—how about those diet boys?), and it's devastating to the bodies that suffer the consequences.

But it ain't nothing compared to where we are going right now. Dieting, starvation, living on powdered concoctions would be considered the highest-quality eating com-

the malnutrition, the chronic malnutrition, that
l in hand with the disease of alcoholism.

ıct: Alcohol blocks the intake of all the essential
vitamins and minerals.

Big statement, and not a good nutritional start. You
can easily figure, with a statement like that leading the
way, that we are probably in a little trouble. I'll throw ya a
bone and tell you that alcohol does that to everyone's
body.

You have a glass of wine with your salad (don't ya hate
women who eat like that?), and the alcohol you drink is
blocking all essential vitamins and minerals. That's not
good, but it's not such a problem when you are having a
couple of drinks a week. So you block a few essential
vitamins and minerals—who cares? Didn't we do that in
the sixties?

But don't ever forget that when we are talking about
alcohol, we are talking about our drinking. Not a glass of
wine with dinner or a beer here or there. That's not what
we do. Remember your liver mitochondria. It ain't ever
about one beer. Never was for me. Four, five, six beers.
Drinking, that's what we are talking about.

Our kind of drinking, our claim to fame, in the beginning stage of our disease, is creating something I (and half
the planet) never, ever thought was happening to me. In
America, the land of plenty, home of the brave, never seen
an airdrop of food, the country with the world's biggest
supermarkets . . . MALNUTRITION?

Let's start with what we already know.
Alcohol is . . .
Fuel with no nutritional value.

Alcohol . . .
Blocks essential vitamins and minerals.

"In addition to its direct, poisonous effects on organs such as the liver, heart, brain, and stomach, alcohol works indirectly as a sort of nutritional vacuum cleaner, sucking up vitamins and minerals and leaving the body with numerous deficiencies."

Alcohol is also . . .
Toxic.
A toxic waste dump.
That's what your body is becoming every time you drink. So put this physical disaster together. You've got, oy, the as-a-tol-da-hyde being produced too fast. Then your acetate is being broken down way too slow, and there is a ton of this stuff floating around your brain. A brain that is being opiated and getting addicted by the second and . . . ?
Something else needs to be added to this mix.

"Every drinking alcoholic is malnourished, meaning that many of his [their] body cells are weakened."

"Nutritional disease in alcoholics is often hidden deep within the cell structure of the body."

"Every alcoholic has nutritional problems."

Malnourished? I'm confused. You don't have scurvy or beriberi. You are not wasting away, don't have the extended belly that you know means malnutrition. You live in the United States, not India. Your teeth and gums are fine. You are not and never will be on the cover of *Time* with huge brown eyes, a tiny thin body, and flies everywhere. You live in a big city or small town, not in Bangladesh. You have two cars or one, or you ride the bus. You ain't walking a hundred miles a day with baskets on your head to gather water. . . . Get real. You may even be lucky enough to be a member of the Junior League (and I'm not sure how much luckier you could get than that). You go to the huge, very super market to do your shopping, with twelve thousand choices of every food under the sun. You buy vats, trailer sizes, of toilet paper and bacon. Red Cross is something you contribute to only once a month (yeah, if any of us did they'd be properly funded). So how on earth could anyone in their right mind suggest that you and I are

   a. malnourished
or
   b. chronically malnourished

Chronic? Do you know what that means?
Chronic means ongoing as opposed to acute. All the time, as opposed to one big stab of.
Chronic, as in years and years of.
Chronic, as in persistent. Chronic, as in always there.
And chronically MALNOURISHED???

• • •

Chronic keeps on keeping on. Chronic is slow and subtle.

Alcoholism is . . .? Slow and subtle. What a coincidence. Or is it?

And think about what chronic does, chronic anything.

Chronic bad marriage. Slowly whittles away your strength. Weakens the foundation. Makes life miserable. Breaks you emotionally, gnaws at you physically, wrecks you.

Living in chronic pain . . .

I called a friend of mine who's been in a wheelchair all her life and asked her about chronic pain . . . What does it do to your life?

"Wait, give me a minute. That's a big question first thing in the morning." (Don't you love her already?)

Chronic pain?

"It limits your planning.

"It limits your hope. Sometimes you'd just as soon die as not.

"It's so present, always there . . . You can't talk about it with anybody after a while because it's boring to them. It's boring to me.

"It clouds your plans for tomorrow.

"It makes you envious of people who don't have it.

"It makes you irritable and cranky, and depending on your personality, it turns you into a martyr or a saint."

Is that brilliant, or what? Can you believe how beautifully that was said? That martyr-or-saint thing sent my brain spinning. Loved it and love you, my friend . . . Thanks for the insight.

Chronic distorts. It distorts our perception of everything. It's like living in a fog.

And chronic malnutrition? Couldn't be good. As a matter of fact, it's got to be really, really bad, and it is. How much of a problem is it connected to your alcoholism? It's a huge problem.

We get malnourished because alcohol is toxic. It irritates, it swells, it interferes with digestion, it blocks vitamin absorption, it dehydrates, it poisons.

We also get malnourished because we drink instead of eat. I'm not talking days without food under the bridge. I'm talking drinking instead of eating in our everyday lives and what it does to our bodies.

We start eating less because we'd rather drink. I did.

Remember, alcohol is fuel. It has calories. So drinking is kinda like eating in the beginning of this disease. You're not that hungry when you've had three or four beers.

That's one way our food intake gets interfered with. Another reason for eating less . . . eating interferes with the high.

If I ate a big dinner, it took me longer to get that fabulous kick, and I had to drink more (not that I wasn't going to drink more anyway) to get to that point where I was happy . . . Drink, drink, drink and then eat to try and absorb some of the alcohol later on that night . . . there's a healthy pattern, ha!

But it's not as if I didn't eat. I mean, when I think *malnourished* I think no food, and I had food, organic food, well-prepared food. I did eat. You do too. Again, remember, I'm talking malnourished while you're driving your BMW. Malnourished while we are running from meeting to meeting. Chronically malnourished and picking the kids up from school on your way to the grocery store. Malnourished and getting together with the girls for one glass (not) of wine. Malnourished and running that studio . . .

Malnourished because we aren't eating as much. We have begun drinking more and more. Malnourished by the toxic effects of alcohol.

Here's how it all happens.

When I was eating my organic low-fat food, things were going on in my digestive system that were interfering with my body's ability to break down the nutrients that I was eating. Nutrients being somewhat important to the human body . . . ???

"Alcohol attacks every organ in the digestive system, it hits them all hard, creating nutritional disaster for the alcoholic."

Nutritional disaster?

See, I told you. We're not talking about a small problem here. We are talking about nutritional disaster.

When I read that statement in Katherine Ketchum and Ann Mueller's fabulous book, *Eating Right to Live Sober,* I turned right to the drawing that explains it all beautifully: Diagram Man!

And you should see this guy . . .

Such a picture on the printed page!

Demo Boy showing me and every other alcoholic out there exactly what's happening every time we drink . . .

• • •

OY, from the esophagus that gets irritated and inflamed, with the lining bent all out of shape . . . to our irritated stomach tissue, with the decreased acids and enzymes and general poor digestion created by alcohol, especially when it comes to protein and minerals, yuck . . . right to the pancreas, where you've got another protein-breakdown issue right along with a fat-breakdown problem going on . . . and there is no talking digestion without including the liver. If ever there was a burden, it's here. Instead of being busy being a liver, your liver is spending its time bailing out, shoveling, getting rid of alcohol, while its normal jobs are being left unattended; and an unattended liver could be nothing but bad (don't have to be a doctor to get there). And as if enough damage wasn't being done, ya got ya common, *ordinaire* small intestine with its damaged cell lining and cilia and all that diarrhea and flushing of nutrients in the urine going on . . . while your large intestine is working either too fast or too slow, dumping nutrients or reabsorbing toxins from the waste materials.

ENOUGH! HAVE YOU EVER???

Who ever thought that all this was going on inside of your body because of the toxic effects of alcohol?

The skin problem you just can't seem to get rid of?

How about that virus that just keeps coming back?

Can't seem to shake this depression?

Well, when you are talking about a deficiency in vitamin C, A, E, and zinc, you might think skin problems.

And about that central nervous system . . . not having enough B_1, B_3, B_6, or B_{12} will absolutely cause a problem.

Go ahead, make sure you don't get enough potassium, calcium, magnesium, or thiamine and see what happens to your heart and blood vessels . . . yipe! And about those bones. Calcium and magnesium rapidly excreted from your body . . .

If it's infections or irregular heartbeats.

Bad bone density or hardening of the arteries.

Depression to diarrhea.

Swollen ankles or reduced sexual function.

Or the "distortion in the size and shape of red blood cells that has been found in 85 percent OF ALL ALCO-HOLICS."

Adrenal malfunction to thyroid problems . . .

We are malnourished and sick. That's the truth.

And sick needs treatment. Come on, go with me there, all you skeptics. Throw me a bone on that one, would ya.

Sick needs treatment. Sick needs strengthening. It does with every other *sick* I know, but for some reason, some strange, unknown, political, cash reason . . . not with alcoholism!!!

With every other disease, it's reasonable to get a second opinion. With alcoholism you are in denial.

It's easy with every other disease to connect the physical with the behavioral . . .

Not quite up to par when you have heart disease?

At the top of your game with cancer? I don't think so.

Diabetic in crisis? Is everything getting done?

Are you functioning brilliantly?

Everything fair?

Reasonable?

Are you managing your life well???

Is it fair to say that may not be happening?

Not alcoholism.

Hmmm, how strange!
Not with alcoholism.

The truth is:

"Sick cells need help; they need to be saturated with nutrients so that they can heal themselves, strengthen their defenses, and go about the business of becoming normal, healthy cells again."

So. Alcoholism, the physical. The destruction. The toxic waste dump that is created inside of your body.

Alcoholism, your sobriety. Healing, curing, treating . . . why nutritional therapy???

Why *not* nutritional therapy, when everyone (from the most innovative, Katherine Ketcham, Ann Mueller, and the likes of them, to the American Dietetic Association, who don't scream *cutting edge*) agrees it's key in helping stop the cravings for alcohol, and supporting the healing for the damage done by the drug you and I are addicted to, the drug that has created mass chaos in our digestive system, our liver, our brains, our cells?

Without the nutritional support and repair that every alcoholic, whether they are wearing the business suit or rags, must have, you are undermining the possibility of sobriety ever being a reality. You are going to be "living" with sick cells, an aching brain, digestive problems, and the effects of chronic malnutrition. Why nutritional support?

How about we change that to a more appropriate question?

• • •

Where the hell has nutritional therapy information been for years and years and years, and why are you still fighting us getting what it is sooooo very obvious that we need to stay sober and heal from our disease, boys???

"Nutritional therapy will lessen the alcoholic's mental and physical discomfort in the first days of treatment and will help his [their] body get started on the long and difficult repair job necessary for continuing good health."

"Such alcoholics typically look better, feel better and are able to commit themselves to lifelong sobriety without the depression, anxiety and craving alcohol that plagues many recovering alcoholics who receive no nutritional therapy."

"Alcohol's massive assault on the structure and functioning of the alcoholic's cells cannot be reversed just by removing alcohol from the body—abstinence alone does not make malnourished cells healthy again."

Now you have it. Something other than "You are so weak willed, can't live honestly, and have some kind of alcoholic emotional makeup that has you drinking again." Think *addictive drug.*

Think *withdrawal.*

Think *craving.*

Think *internal destruction.*

Think *sick.*

Think *cellular damage.*

Think, *Need repair.*

Think, *Need treatment . . .*

Think about alcoholism differently!

Think differently about why you haven't been able to stay stopped in the past.

I'll ask you. When you have stopped before, how'd you feel? Healthy, strong, free of alcohol?

I didn't. I thought about alcohol a hundred times a day. I craved the stuff. Sure, for the first couple of days after the "disaster" that caused the promise to stop again, I was firmly planted in my conviction. Then a couple of days into never drinking again for as long as I lived . . . I was drinking.

A Space for Healing

What nutritional support will give you is a space—a space for healing. It's a given with this disease like no other I know: there's no room for healing, no room for treatment . . . no place to get well.

We have been poisoned, had massive damage going on inside our bodies and brain. All of us are physically sick, some of us are realllllllllllllllly sick, sick, sick . . . You stop drinking and it's just, *Go on, back to work with ya, get up and do all the things you normally do.*

Get back to work.

Deal with the kids.

Pay those bills.

Come on . . .

Gut it up and get on with it . . .

I know people who can't get through a day with a damn headache, let alone a liver that's got all kinds of cellular damage going on.

The flu puts most of us out for a few days—and a poisoned brain isn't something that needs just a little attention and care?

If you've got a stomach ache that's reason enough to make you lie in bed and moan . . . I had malnutrition and I can't get an ounce of understanding . . . I get judgment and disgust?

Hey, someone you know breaks their hip. Do you tell 'em, "Get up and dance, you lazy swine"?

Get up.

Get in the car.

Come on, get on with it.

What's the matter with you?

MOVE IT, WEENIE BOY WITH THE WALKER . . .

Would you say to someone who was suffering from a degenerative disease, "You MS weak-willed piece of junk"?

I don't think so . . . but when it comes to being crippled by this disease, that's exactly how we are treated. Interesting, don't ya think? Making these connections is fascinating. Figuring out the huge holes in current recovery think and nontreatment is necessary. Seeing how differently we are treated and why is important, important stuff. Not to point fingers or accuse, but for you and me (alcoholic) to understand, update, include forty-plus years of research into our thinking—and to change the thinking, the judgment, the incorrect everything that's been going on around our disease. You and me redefining recovery. Who else is going to do it?

Yes, we did it to ourselves. We had a drink like you had a drink.

We all did it to ourselves ('cause the whole world drinks). We are encouraged, lured, seduced, pressured, and supported into doing it . . . $600 million a year in advertising makes sure of that. That's not an excuse, that's a fact.

Because of our genetic makeup, you and I got sick.

Rather than the "you piece-of-junk alky" thinking that has gotten us nowhere in the last thirty-nine years—since the AMA established our disease as a physical disease then just kinda left it there—how about the concept of learning more about what it is you and I have and the wonderful treatments that have been available (and not offered by your doctor or any recovery meeting you'll ever walk into) for years. The ointment we need to heal the wounds.

It's time to get nutritional therapy, there is no question about it anymore.

"The abstained alcoholic will continue to suffer protracted withdrawal symptoms till the healing process is complete, without nutritional therapy he [they] may never fully recover."

I've seen it. Above and beyond all the wonderful testimonials of all the people I've spoken with who have had the privilege of nutritional therapy, I've had the most amazing example of sober life with and sober life without, the living example in my own family.

My mother was sober for over a decade before she died. God bless her and the strength she had in staying that way . . .

She lived one day at a time and hung on through the depression, the anxiety, the coffee, the ciggies, the exhaustion, the blood sugar to her toes, and as God is my witness, I don't know how she did it!

I don't know how or why anyone would have to live that way. But she did.

And my brother, Mark. Sober with nutritional therapy. Totally different daily existence. That's what's kept him sober, because without it he wouldn't be. He tried my mother's way and couldn't do it.

Now that I understand how difficult it is to live with diseased cells that get no treatment, a glucose-deprived brain, digestive problems, depression, anxiety, and exhaustion, I have a new and enormous respect for what my mother said to me one week before she died of lung cancer.

She'd had her esophagus radiated, so she couldn't eat.

They were giving her an IV of iron, so she couldn't go to the bathroom.

Clogging to death, starving to death was basically what was happening.

At sixty-something pounds she looked at me and said, "Funny, I really feel like a beer."

It had been years since she'd even made a reference to alcohol.

I said, "Ma, come on . . . have one. Why not?"

Her answer to my lame attempt to try and get something inside her, some food, some something (my thinking was, *Who cares? If you want it, have it*) . . .

Her answer was:

"I will die sober."

And she did, one week later.

I've got a question at this point in our discussion. If not drinking for an alcoholic is as intolerable as we now know it can be and the bottle is the only and instant relief, why wouldn't you pick it up?

Another thread in the "Why can't you just stay stopped, you irresponsible piece of junk?" thinking.

You are not getting any other treatment for your disease, and the solution to the pain you are in is on every street corner. It's being shoved down your throat every time you get on a plane, every afternoon at five, being served at every luncheon. It's being served everywhere. Why wouldn't you pick it up when you are hurting?

Think about it, all you nonalcoholics. You've got the worst migraine headache of all time for weeks, and the medicine that will wipe it out is being offered to you constantly.

You'd have trouble refusing it, wouldn't ya?

Is it too much to ask that the physical suffering, the damage and destruction that's been done, be repaired.

We could even go so far as to suggest that it be included in one of the steps, maybe one of the first steps, since it has a whole lot to do with staying stopped . . . ?

"An overwhelming majority of habitual alcohol and drug abusers were suffering from severe metabolic and nutritional imbalances. When these conditions were corrected, these patients usually experienced sharply diminished needs for getting high by artificial means."

Even the American Dietetic Association has figured it out, and it takes them a while. (Still telling us that the best source of protein is beef? Come on, how about the saturated fat, cholesterol, and the chemical waste dump that domesticated beef has become in our country? Meat and antibiotics, you've heard it. Chicken loaded with pus . . . Sure, just take twelve seconds and have a look at what goes into our domesticated meat before you eat it . . . Get ready, you'll be grossed out—grossed out? Hard to believe I just used that term.)

Back to the American Dietetic Association . . .

They did a study in 1991 about nutritional imbalances in alcoholics, and guess what they found?

Thirty-eight patients.

Eighteen did the standard recovery thing.

Twenty received nutritional counseling along with the standard recovery thing.

"Those receiving nutritional therapy experienced less cravings for alcohol."

Over and over again, when you do the slightest investigation into nutritional support and recovering from the

155

disease of alcoholism, you see that alcoholics who get nutritional support

experience fewer cravings for alcohol
experience fewer symptoms for hypoglycemia
and are able to abstain from alcohol consumption
 more easily

We begin to heal so much of the damage that has been done.

That's what happened to me when I got the nutritional support I needed. That's what happened to my brother.

That's not what happened to my mother.

!¦!!/

Failing

The really sad part about you and me not getting this information sooner is the unnecessary beating our self-esteem took every time we stopped drinking and "failed." The fear that we have been living in is unnecessary. The self-loathing that goes on because we can't stick to our promise to ourselves, the wife, the husband, the boyfriend, the kids, your mother, your father, whoever is involved in our promise to quit this time ("I really mean it, no more," and then . . .) is unnecessary.

The AMA, Madison Avenue, the American government, the liquor lobbies, and the alcohol industry are responsible for that pain and suffering, just like the tobacco industry is responsible for the lung cancer created by the product they developed and advertised as sexy, sophisticated, just plain fun to do. Current recovery thinking is responsible for refusing to make the bio-chemical connection that is imperative for successful treatment of your disease, i.e., your sobriety.

Until they take the responsibility they need to take and move toward changing it (which I have a feeling is going to be a while), you are going to have to do it yourself, because not many people around you are going to be able to understand, support, encourage, or help you in this new thinking.

Recently I have had the opportunity to see the love, the support, the persistence, and the pure intentions behind that current recovery thinking. There is no way I would suggest that we get rid of what has worked for some. The problem seems to be in reconciling the decades of research, the millions it doesn't work for, and the complete lack of treatment for the disease of alcoholism that is the reality of current recovery thinking today. Why not include:

> group support *and* nutritional therapy
> accountability *and* treating a glucose-deprived
>   brain
> surrender *and* balancing blood sugar
> forgiveness *and* vitamins
> getting a sponsor *and* having a whole meal

Increase the power of the healing. Up the stats. Help millions more recover.

Open the books, boys, and stop saying you don't know anything about it anymore.

• • •

Six months ago, I would have said:

"You can't say you don't know anything about this anymore. We are getting educated. The facts can't be hidden."

Now I say to you, the alcoholic: "Learn this. Share this. Take this to your meeting and open the discussion. Get the books, start the talk, get the vitamins, eat real, whole, healing food, and tell everyone you know about it."

I was the child who was the victim of the industries who've been keeping this from us for years, and I have a right to be pissed. So do you, adult children of fellow alcoholics, but let's get past that and get on with the healing, the truth, the light, the way . . .

And let's begin by once and for all clearing up the behavior-of-an-alcoholic discussion and connecting it with what's really happening, the progression of your progressive disease.

Behavior

I remember distinctly when my drinking changed. It was my pattern changing that I noticed first. It was one of the beginning signs, the initial awareness that there was a shift from the kind of drinking everyone does to something different, mine.

Years ago. Owning and running my exercise studio alone. Teaching twenty-six classes a week because I couldn't afford the payroll to actually have teachers.

Cleaning the joint. Someone had to scrub the toilets, clean the floors, and make the place look pretty—and I did.

Working, working, working, inside and outside my home. Running a business, a home, and a family. And once a week—not always, but if I was "lucky"—I'd get to sit down with some friends, have a few beers, and relax. No big deal, and loads and loads of fun. Certainly nothing wrong with it (and remember, I could hold mine better than most). Who would ever, ever think there was something wrong with having a few beers once a week, especially when you are working as hard as I was? Nobody— not me, anyway! Nothing irresponsible about it.

No symptoms of any disease.

Nothing unusual at all. No understanding of the cellular changes that were going on inside my body every time I took a sip of alcohol.

Alcoholic??? What, are you out of your mind? Never even a thought given . . .

My mitochondria? Why would I think about it. The only thought of being alcoholic or reference to it was when someone was "irresponsibly" drinking, and I was seeing that all around me. Brother Mark ring a bell? My brother was a walking drinking disaster at that point in my life. My having a drink once a week and my brother, Mark's, drinking—there was no comparison!

If anything, it was nothing but confirmation of how normal I was and how alcoholic he was. I was soooo far from irresponsible anything, so who knew?

Stage one of our disease has you thinking that nothing is wrong. Drinking more than most but handling it better. No clue about the cellular changes going down in your liver. Never a thought given to the opiated brain, the addicted brain, the beginning of malnutrition, as-a-tol-da-hyde, or acetate . . . who ever thought about it? But that's exactly what's going on.

Stage two of our disease is about frequency, quantity, shame, lies, guilt, and fear . . .

At this stage of the deadly game, it's two for one (pardon the happy-hour pun). Progression in frequency and quantity, plus an extra bonus thrown in—the emotional, spiritual, and personal crashing that works so well in bringing us to our knees. It's happening all at once, and you don't have a clue yet what's going on.

I don't know exactly when—there was no real occasion or particular event—and I don't remember why, but I do remember noticing a couple of things.

First, for a couple of weeks in a row, I was "getting together with some friends" every three days instead of every five. *Getting together* isn't exactly right. My having a few beers was getting together with the stuff that had to get done.

The "Let's get together" reason to have a few began to mix with the business meeting, or doing the payroll (I was building two things at once, a business and a disease), or a teacher training . . . whatever it was, we'd have a few while we did it. It was usually me that suggested we have a drink. You wanna know how I knew for sure something was different? The length of time between the days when I felt horrible (the inevitable morning after the gathering) was shorter and shorter. That's what I noticed first.

I was busy, very busy.

I'm talking getting the kids off to school, making the beds, organizing what's for dinner, running to the studio to teach three classes back to back, and then handling the business before the kids had to be picked up. You gotta have energy to do that. There are no days off when you're working in and outside the house. The millions of women in this country working full-full-time know that.

When I didn't feel "right," it really tilted me. If it took me just a little longer to pull myself together in the morning, it threw my whole day off . . . so I noticed when things weren't right. That's what jolted me at first. Something was being taken from me—energy, endurance—something I needed to function doing ten times the work and getting one third the pay and credit (pardon my personal political platform moment). Instead of having five or six very productive days, then a slow morning (the once-a-week-gather-with-the-friends-drinking-night morning after), I began to notice that I was having two or three good, strong, productive days and then a slow morning. Silly me and millions of us out there, I thought I was just tired. Perfectly normal to have some slow starts, as busy as I was . . . but something inside of me (just like your something inside) knew that this interesting energy-slowdown, not-feeling-too-well thing was connected to my drinking increasing.

A glimpse of the problem, but who was gonna see it then? It wasn't such a problem. (When I tell you I was productive, I'm not kidding—books, TV, radio, infomercials, teaching, the boys, the house, the marriage. So when I say slow start I'm talking still doing more by five in the afternoon than most people do in a week. It's not as if I was sofa-bound by this energy zapper, and besides, it was big, big, fun and perfectly normal.)

Getting high is fun, that's why people do it. If drugs weren't fun they would not be so popular. Drinking is fun. How could you ever tell anyone it isn't? Having a few is not only normal. It is a social rite of passage.

• • •

But something was happening to me.

My willpower wasn't changing. My disease was progressing.

"The alcoholic reacts physically in an abnormal way to alcohol, and his [their] disease begins long before he [they] behaves or thinks like an alcoholic . . . in months or years, the cells will have been so altered by alcohol that the alcoholic's behavior and thought processes will be affected. Then the disease will no longer be hidden and the alcoholic will clearly be in trouble with alcohol."

This is where the scary, scary stuff "starts" to happen. Here's where the behavioral changes sneak in and shock you every time they "happen."

Sneaking drinks??? Never. Me sneak a drink? Why would I? I am an adult. I don't have a religious or moral problem with having a beer . . . What's going on when I find myself chugging a beer alone in the break room of the studio before I take one out to everyone in the meeting, along with the one for me . . . after I've chugged the first one?

Stopping off to grab a drink on the way home becoming a normal event—when did that happen?

You're at the party and you make sure you are the bartender. Ahhhh, that rush of excitement when you are at a drinking event—where'd that come from? And the drinks you make, stronger than you ever have before. You put a little extra in "just in case." Just in case what? I'm telling you, I heard those words in my brain (we'll talk later about those voices we hear).

How about sitting down and having a couple before the event, whatever the event may be? They call it "pre-drinking." I called it normal during this stage of my disease.

It never ends and never gets easier to think about . . .

The thought of how fast I started to drink the drinks . . . gulping the alcohol.

Adding a little hard liquor to the beer once in a while, so it was one beer and a scotch on the rocks . . .

Bammo! All of a sudden you are drinking more than you ever imagined. Six beers every time you get together with friends. The whole bottle of wine. Drinking more often and more of it, and living with all the side effects of drinking too much. There's no way you can drink more often without it seeping into areas of your life that you never, ever thought it would.

And when it does, the guilt and the justifications. You know, you are living it. At this stage . . .

"The alcoholic's guilt, depression, self-loathing, and despair are understandable reactions to the bewildering and mysterious inability to stop the ravages of drinking."

Who would have thought that you'd drink and drive as much as you do now?

It became perfectly normal for me to grab a beer and jump in the car when I was driving my kids somewhere.

163

I remember going to the store to get dinner, takeout Chinese, and picking up some beer . . . nothing unusual. So what? But when did it become normal for me to open a beer the minute I got into the car? Never thinking to wait till I got home. Didn't matter who was driving, I'm having a beer. When did that happen? When did I start going to the store first, so I would have a beer to drink on the way to the restaurant to pick up the takeout, and a couple on the way home? Before dinner even started, I'm on my fifth beer. Truth is, I couldn't wait any longer to have that beer. Needed it? Had to have it immediately?

I wasn't getting up in the morning thinking about alcohol, yet.

I never drank during the day, yet.

Nothing about my business was being interfered with, yet. That all happens soon enough. What was really digging its claws in at this point was the physiological development in my disease.

The behavioral, shameful hell starts to build right along with the physiological and you don't have a clue it's happening—but your disease is in full swing.

The cells of our central nervous system are becoming addicted to alcohol.

Our mitochondria are adapting to alcohol.

Our brain is addicted.

Our bodies are being poisoned . . .

We are building our disease.

During this stage, the social and psychological web starts to get built, and this combination is deadly. A vial of "weakness-of-will" poison is being added to the physical brew that you didn't know until now was/is happening inside your body.

• • •

This is where we start to believe that there is something wrong with us. Way before you ever hear the incorrect, weakness-of-will argument from standard recovery programs you've already spent a long, long time dancing around it, hiding from it, keeping others (everyone in your life) from discovering it, and have started to believe it yourself . . . DANGER, WILL ROBINSON!

Because unless you are total slime (and there is total slime out there—most of us aren't), you are bothered, aware of, uncomfortable with the behaviors that are happening as a result of your disease. Driving drunk. Not something anyone I know is comfortable with. And driving drunk repeatedly, no matter how many times you say you won't do it again (and it happens over and over again), that's enough to scare the hell out of anyone.

Being hungover a couple of times a week—that's not anything people I know take lightly. It worries them. It worried me. I was scared. I felt as if something was happening to me, and it was. The truth is, most people are ashamed or embarrassed when they make a fool of themselves because they had too much to drink. And when all of this stuff happens over and over again, no matter how many times you say, "Never again"—judge yourself? They do. I did. You do.

I know you are ashamed of your inability to control your drinking.

There's no question that you are afraid that there is something wrong with you.

You definitely start to wonder if you are self-sabotaging.

Maybe you don't love everyone enough?

Is your life not important enough to you?

Are you an irresponsible slut?

What deep, dark, psychological secret is lurking in your life that is "causing" you to drink too much?

You and I let that thinking in way before we ever get to the group.

All this is going on while your body is getting sicker and sicker. Every cell, your liver, your brain not doing too well under the strain of this poison, this drug that is causing havoc in your body.

The questions that triggered in my brain for days after (not so long, because, remember, my pattern was already set in stone—it was only a couple more days "after" that I was drinking again) were far more painful than any hangover could ever be. I was physically, emotionally, and spiritually sick.

How can anyone who loves another human being as much as I love my kids do something sooooo irresponsible?

How could I have driven home so drunk?

What happened?

Why did I do that?

God, I could have killed myself or someone else!

What an irresponsible asshole, when my kids depend on me.

OK, no more. Never again. That's it.

Week after week, time after time, the plans are laid, the boundary setting done.

!"!/

Setting Boundaries

Setting boundaries. It's a good thing to do in every area of our lives? You gotta do it in relationships, with your work, with the kids, and it's a must if you have to keep drinking. Because that's what this is about now, how to keep drinking. You are no longer in the driver's seat of this bus; it's the addictive voice, the brain that's gotta have the glucose, the opium den that needs someone to come in and suck on the pipe or it's gonna close down.

This is a good place to look back upon to get some answers about your disease, or to look at right now, if you are still in it. All you gotta do is ask one question. Here's one way to know you are different from Joe or Josephine. If anything were causing so much confusion and pain in their life, they'd quit.

They would be thrilled to hear that the cause of all the suffering, guilt, hangovers, shame, and pain was drinking. Because if it's coming from the drinking, there would be, and is, an easy, easy solution to ending the suffering. Stop drinking.

That would be good news to the average Joe or Josephine . . . is it good news to you?

For most people that would be logical and exactly what happens . . . but it never, ever, ever dawned on me. I didn't even consider never drinking. All I spent my time doing is trying to figure out how I could.

We have less choice now in stage two. Our disease is firmly rooted, taking over our body, brain, and life.

It's a painful stage, this stage two. Not physically painful. Other than the hangover, nausea, shame, guilt, and fear, you can't feel the agony your liver and brain are in

. . . that silent torture that's going on inside. The pain is in the glimpses of the problem, your drinking problem, the glimpses of light that you get during stage two.

It's when you really begin to feel a little addicted. When you become really aware of the fact that you can't stop, because you haven't been able to and, at this point, you've said you are going to thousands of times. And no matter what you do, it just keeps "happening."

Here's where you really start trying to get a grip, and you find out that alchohol has got you in its grip . . .

So let's get back to boundary setting. You want a really good tool for checking if something's wrong? Check your rules. Have a look at the boundaries you've set around your drinking—you know, all those regulations you've set down to ensure you'll be able to keep drinking.

Check it out. Have a look at how your life is broken down at this "stage" of the game. Drinking and living. It's become two separate activities. How are you going to live your life and do all the things you need to do AND drink?

You make up rules, like I made up rules, like all alcoholics make up rules.

Rule

I'll never drink again when I know that I have to pick up the kids.

Just think about that for a second. My kids are with me every day of my life. I am responsible for getting them to, teaching them how, and helping them get there, every-

where. And I'm not going to drink when they are involved??? Look at that logic and you'll clearly see the world
that an addict lives in. Twisted thinking that supports one
thing, continued drinking . . .

Rule

Never before three in the afternoon.

Can't happen, no drinking before three . . . And when it's
a Sunday barbecue at the lake (I say that like I've ever in
my life been to a Sunday barbecue by the lake . . . I don't
come from an eat-by-the-lake family), you aren't gonna
have a beer, glass of wine, or one of those tub-made mar-
garitas they've got cooking up?

Rule

Nothing but beer.

Love this logic. As long as it's not "hard" liquor? Only
beer from now on?

Rule

**One beer, one glass of water, to make sure I don't
drink too fast.**

The only reason you're making up the rules is because
it's out of control.

Do you think a nonalcoholic has to make up a rule that they won't drink before three in the afternoon or with their kids in the car? No.

How about someone who isn't addicted even having to think about waiting till they get home to have a beer? It's a non-issue.

¡!!!¡

Alcoholism is a progressive disease, and one of the first "progressions" you are going to become all too familiar with is the progressive scenario that begins with "I'm never drinking again."

You stop drinking.

For good.

And you start.

And you stop again. Forever, that's it . . .

And you start.

And you stop again for a little longer.

And you start.

And it just keeps going, the progression of stopping and starting and stopping and starting, and . . . failure.

Failure.

I didn't know how to stop drinking.

"It" was getting out of "control," and I had to find a way to still do it and not get caught or die . . . both would have been equally devastating at that point!

Because it wasn't just the frequency that was increasing in the stage-two full-swing stage; it was and will always be (so very textbook) the urgency to drink.

Suddenly you become more and more aware of the need to have it there. I'm not talking an urge to drink like an urge to push the baby out. This disease is much more subtle than that. It's a need to make sure that alcohol is just there, at the event, around.

When someone suggests a get-together, you will always be the one making sure the booze is there. Bring it, suggest it, jump in the car and make the run for it . . . At this stage of my disease my meetings in the studio always included a drink, and I was always the one to suggest it and usually the one to go get it.

The teachers would have one or two. After a hard day of wellness, I'd have four or five.

My awareness of my pattern had a three-dimensional element to it . . . I clearly remember walking into the studio over and over again holding the grocery bag with the beer in it . . . I became acutely aware of how common the sight of me holding a grocery bag at five in the afternoon was becoming to my clients . . .

The sounds of the classes that were being taught.

Walking in as if it wasn't the third time that week that I'd brought in a couple of six-packs.

It's so embarrassing and sad to think back on some of the things I'd do to make it look casual, normal, like maybe there was tonight's dinner inside the bag.

I became all too familiar with and aware of the ritual of unpacking the beer . . .

Trying to get it done before anyone walked in so that it would just be there, as opposed to me putting it there again.

I'd put them away quickly, grabbing a couple for myself. Even arranging the bottles so it didn't look as if any had been taken, like I'd just unpacked them and left, not unpacked them and grabbed a few because I needed a couple of beers to finish up some work before the meeting began.

Then two or three when the meeting got under way. (You can clearly see the need for more than a six-pack . . . I've already downed five myself—what's left for anyone else who wants a beer? So from now on, it's two or three six-packs. Progression, progression, progression all around me, and I didn't see the Mack truck coming for nothing . . .)

And don't forget the unwinding after the meeting. Another couple of beers just before we tie it up and I'm on my way home . . .

Homework.

Dinner.

Finish up some work.

A couple of loads of laundry.

The kids, bath, ready for bed, and up at 5 A.M. to begin again!

A little tougher than it used to be, this getting up at dawn to run the business. Must be getting older?

Once in a while, I'd arrange for another teacher to take my 6 A.M. class that I'd been teaching forever.

Oh my God, what an irresponsible jerk! This is my business I worked my butt off to make successful. Having another teacher take my class because I'd had too much to drink the night before . . .

There were days when I would go home and take a nap in the middle of the day . . . What kind of businesswoman was I?

Driving drunk a good couple of times a week . . . God,
what could be worse, you piece of shit?
How many runs to the liquor store? Junk, irresponsible,
stupid junk (finish this sentence with the words
"that's what you are").
Damn it, I drank too much again last night. What's the
matter with you? Where's your discipline? It's enough.
Get a grip.

Start feeding this junk into your brain over and over
again for a couple of years and see what happens. You are
what you eat, and you certainly are what you think . . . My
brain went on a steady emotional diet of complete junk—
fear, confusion, disappointment, and shame—while my
body (on the outside) looked better than it ever had. I
had no clue what was happening on the inside of my
body, but I knew what was happening on the inside of my
heart/head. I didn't know my brain was in physical agony,
but my heart was. There are not many places I've ever
been (and you could imagine I've been a few) where I
felt as bad as that place felt. Just damn scared and confused.

Sound familiar? Are you there yet? I'm telling you the
truth when I say it's the most traveled road (we all experience so much of the same old same old and feel soooooo
alone while we are doing it). There are millions of us walking the same path.

I wasn't dealing with any of this stuff in any other area
of my life . . . Are you kidding? Remember, I was building
a multimillion-dollar business . . . a national reputation
and human beings, my children. Things were great, better

than they had ever been. I wish I had known then that none of the shame and guilt I was feeling had anything to do with what was really going on. I wish I had known the truth about my disease.

What is happening in our disease is not different from what happens with all disease—the infection, the complication of a physical disease, the debilitating effects that any disease would have on your life. Illness interferes. No question. It limits. It creates fear and uncertainty.

Alcoholism is no exception. Except that this degenerative disease is cloaked in enormous amounts of shame, fear, and guilt because of the ignorance and incorrect information that has put us there and kept us there . . . That's when you've got the real poison going on.

You are in big, big trouble when you start judging yourself. Living in the desperate fear of this disease does affect us. When you feel that excitement, the anticipation (sounds completely exaggerated to anyone who isn't alcoholic, but you know what I'm talking about, that rush when you know the kick is just a couple of sips away) that builds every time you get next to the chance to drink. It feels shameful.

The party, the meeting, the gathering, whatever it is . . . the reason to drink takes first place, the people and the event take second place. The activity of drinking becomes number one.

If you look closely and honestly at what happened back then or may be happening right now, you'll be able to see and understand that you are not a shitty friend or a horrible person (which is what most of us are left feeling and thinking). You are in a really dangerous, scary part of your very well developed, firmly planted disease, and I'm sorry to say that if you keep drinking, this is only the beginning —there is sooo much more pain, so many barriers that you thought you'd never cross, because once you are here, as I said to a friend of mine at this stage of my disease, without ever saying the word *alcoholic,* "Something is changing. It sounds weird, but I feel as if there is a cellular change in my body. Something is different inside of me." . . . If only I understood then what I was a year from understanding—how fast, how vicious, how completely controlling this damn disease is!

My last year of drinking took me to places I never thought I'd go. Not just to irresponsible actions—drunk driving, falling down, making a fool of myself—but to a place of shame and fear that was far worse than the external signs of my disease.

My shame may have been somewhat compounded by the fact that I'm nationally known for fitness. And my confusion and inability (and the fear of everyone else's inability) to reconcile *fitness expert* and *drunk* (reread the truth and you'll understand) was highlighted because I have worked hard, am good at what I do, am financially responsible for my family and others, and was afraid of what would happen when "they knew."

But that was only a very small part of what I know now to be the shame that we all feel, the shame that this disease breeds in, the fertilizer for alcoholism. The shame that keeps us locked into our disease is truly much more connected to our ignorance about this disease.

We can move mountains to eliminate that by getting the facts about treatment for the disease of alcoholism.

The information I didn't have supported the hiding and the fear.

Not knowing anything about my brother's, my mother's, or my biochemistry absolutely left me with nothing but all the "character" reasons why . . .

Why I was doing all the things I was doing.

Why I just couldn't gut it up and solve the problem.

Why I couldn't stop and stay stopped.

Now that I understand, I'm not afraid anymore. In fact, I embrace my disease because I understand it. I look forward to sharing what I consider to be the most transforming information I've ever heard—information that could potentially reduce at least one of the statistics: alcohol is the largest killer of young adults in our country!

This information gives us more than anger to solve the drunk-driving problem in our country. It gives us facts, a treatment, a way to solve the problem.

This really is an opportunity to literally save lives, and if all it takes to make that possible is to tell the truth . . . then here it is.

I am an alcoholic, and if you are too, let's get you treatment for your disease.

Prescription . . . The Cure

The hardest part about learning is unlearning. Go, Gloria Steinem, go. True as true can be, and absolutely the case when it comes to the disease of alcoholism. Unlearning what you think you know, getting rid of all the junk that you've heard or believed, not listening to the cave dwellers or the flat-world believers, who are all over the place desperately trying to convince you that you really are the moral leper that they want you to believe you are . . . that's gonna be tough.

Curing the disease of alcoholism isn't tough.

"For most of us, quitting drinking is no worse than a mild or moderate case of flu. It's no biggie."

I know, I know, there's a whole lot of drama surrounding quitting drinking. Hitting the worst gutter of your life? With your head between your legs you are supposed to know that you can't control your life. Rehab, shame, nonfunctioning, failed again, no self-control, problems, problems, problems.

You are supposed to be completely incapable of doing it alone. There's gonna be someone that you have to call every twelve seconds, gutters to fall into, lots of pain and problems along the way, right?

Wrong. When you have the right biochemical help, the correct information, the truth about your disease, it isn't difficult to stop drinking. When you have the tools of the sober trade and you understand how to work them and apply them to your life. It isn't difficult to stay stopped.

Sober isn't difficult, and NO DOUBT ABOUT IT, it is the best thing on the planet. That's the truth, and here's the way, here's how, here's your plan.

The Plan

Said it before and I'll say it again—what's gonna be different this time?

You are going to stop drinking, and maybe it could

work again for however long you've stopped in the past. Then what? As sure as you've been before that it was "over" ("no more," "never gonna do it again," the twelve thousand times that you have quit) . . . What? This time is gonna make it different? What's the plan gonna be to take you where you "couldn't" go before? Staying stopped. The sobriety plan. What are you going to do to ensure success in sobriety this time?

Look at any other important event in our lives. College (yeah, like I know anything about that), first job, family, first house, I don't know—every Ozzie and Harriet thing you can think of—and there's usually a ton of planning and thought that goes into it all. We organize, we plan. A lot of thought goes into these important decisions and events in our life.

There's a process to go through to make sure it's done right, backup plans in case it doesn't work. Well organized. Planned. Strategized. You work it.

If you decided tomorrow that you were going to run a marathon, would ya ever think of just getting up on the day of the race and saying, "All righty, this is the big one. Today I'm gonna do it," and actually going out and running it?

No training.

Nothing different in your diet.

No focus.

Just putzing along in your regular habits and lifestyle till the day of the race, and then hoping like hell you'll get through it when the time comes.

Do that and:

a. Drop dead.
b. Last about twelve seconds.

c. Don't bother, 'cause when you take a look around and see what you're up against, you'll know you don't have a chance in hell of making it.

Call me simple. Call me the spouter of psychobabble (one of the favorite criticisms of doctors who aren't selling as many books as motivational speakers). Call me whatever you want, but I've got a question for you, the question I asked myself when I said for the fifty thousandth time that I wasn't going to ever drink again because I was "sick of this stuff," "didn't want it in my life anymore," "wasn't willing to harm my family," "didn't want to hurt myself or anybody else," and, "That was it. Never, ever again."

What have you done differently on the fifty thousandth time you quit?

Are you any more committed this time than you were last week? Have you just "had it" a little more this time, and that's gonna make it different when the urge hits tomorrow or five minutes from now? Is something just going to be there for you now that wasn't there before? I'm confused!

Do we have a clue why, when, what is gonna help you stay stopped? Any plan? Any clue how?

If you need to accomplish a goal, sobriety being a good one if you are alcoholic, then shouldn't you pull in everything you've got? You see, that's what this book, this information, this discussion on current recovery thinking is suggesting. Add to. Let's give people who want to stop drinking everything they need. The last forty-plus years of research; a strong, healthy, well-balanced body; the meetings; the steps that can help, combined with the information that could help millions more . . . nothing wrong with that!

Because I say, if you've ever planned in your life, wouldn't it be now? Researched? Buying a house more important than saving your own life? I don't think so! Résumé . . . dress for success? Something that needs to be studied more than how you are going to live or die? No chance!

Do we or don't we love too much? Who cares?

Who cares about anything now except how you are going to get past the next day, hour, minute?

You may not be training for a twenty-six-mile marathon, you may only be concerned with the next sixty seconds of not drinking, but it's a marathon just the same because the end result would be to win. If your biggest fear is the next hour, afternoon, or the next cocktail party, fair enough. You need a little help and a clear, clear understanding of exactly what you are going to do when the desire to drink, the justification out the wazoo, the addicted voice inside your brain, convinces you that this whole not drinking thing is really just drama and that it was really never that

bad
irresponsible
poisonous
sloppy
frightening
hopeless

because, believe me, it's gonna happen. The next cocktail party is right around the corner, and the first couple are a little scary till you know what to do.

The most unbelievably difficult thing in your life right now may be entertaining the idea of never, ever, for the rest of your life having another drink. OK. Stay there and know that you are sooo far from alone. We all feel that way the first couple of times we look at it. It is that big and it is that frightening, but it ain't real.

I got a glimpse of something similar years ago that helped me years later, at this stage of the game I never thought I'd be playing, the sober game.

Doing the same thing over and over again and expecting different results, the definition of *insanity,* or dieting? Again I go where you don't understand how I could possibly go. In the middle of such an important discussion on how to stop drinking forever, I'm back to . . . my weight loss . . . but I promise you, the two are so connected that I have to go there. So come with me.

Dieting. Failure. Dieting. Failure. Garland, Texas. Failure. Dieting. Losing weight and gaining it back. Garland, Texas. Big failure. Something wrong with me. Just can't seem to stick to it. Don't know what to do. How come I can't just do it???

I'd drink the shakes (the chalky upper and lower GI mixtures with a bit of strawberry flavoring thrown in) for months, living on liquid, and "do well" for a while. Then I'd put a morsel of food in my mouth and bingo! Blowfish!

Feeling like the biggest loser in town (and the only one until I found out that 98 percent of us that go on these things fail), I was as big as a house (one-hundred-plus pounds overweight) and as miserable as they (the cat's mother?) can get.

How many times did I get up and swear that I was going on a diet? A hundred thousand?

Definitely every Monday morning. Absolutely just before any big occasion. Every year when summer was right around the corner . . .

And where was the plan, and what was it? What was I going to do to make the difference at that moment in front of the fridge with the food? Where was the "motivation," "strength," "desire to live a healthy life" going to come from?

How many times did I get up and swear that I wasn't going to drink again? A hundred thousand times.

And what was the plan? What was going to be different this time? Where was the whatever it was that was going to make me not pick up the beer going to come from?

Seeing the connection? I told ya, stick with me, kid, and I'll connect it for ya!

Like every woman (the primary victims of the diet industry—pardon, but I had to) who has battled weight in her life, when it came to losing it, over and over again in my life I said it, I did it, and it worked—for a while. Then it "happened" every time. Failure. I ended up right back where I'd started. Just as fat, if not fatter, and always, always, always feeling worse about myself. My inability to "stick with it." Something wrong with me (and the other 98 percent of us who do fail—the diet industry's stats, not mine!). I was the one who kept failing, and there was nothing I seemed to be able to do about it. Which made me a failure.

Well—long story short—I found out that I wasn't failing.

The system that I was working, dieting, was one of the biggest scams out there. I found out that there was a solution to the problem of that extra 133 pounds I was schlepping around and that there was nothing magical or mystical about getting it off, keeping it off, and looking and feeling better than I've ever felt (and still do) in my life.

The system, dieting, sets you, me, and the rest of the world up for failure. It is deliberate. It is profit driven. You are talking about some mighty powerful boys when you talk about the industries that want you fat, that want you to keep failing, to get sick, so they can . . .

> be the gym you sign up with
> be the doctor who saves you
> be the "diet" program that you have a lifetime
>   membership with
> be the ones that applaud you each week when you
>   lose a pound or two
> advertise to you at the first of every year

That promise . . .

Well, it's a false promise. There is a lifestyle that leads to being lean, strong, and healthy, and it's got nothing at all to do with dieting . . . Well documented, easy to get the info, but then to apply it???

Years ago I'm asking myself the question, what's going to make a difference when I go to the fridge?

Why am I all of a sudden going to pick the high-volume, low-fat, high-quality food as opposed to the instant shake, the quick and easy (not the solution to the problem, but definitely the instant answer to the symptom), the big chunk of cheesecake, 'cause "What the hell, I've already blown it"? Why will I stick to what is going to get me the end result I want and what I had committed to just days before?

Cut to:

Years later, when I find myself asking the same question about alcoholism! What do you think?

Glad to have had the experience to call on. Thrilled to be able to write about it years later in a book about alcoholism. A very, very valid and important part of healing, solving the problem instead of treating the symptoms. Yes, yes, yes . . . but digesting this little life lesson standing at the fridge staring at the beer as opposed to the cheesecake and realizing that there wasn't a plan AGAIN was not fun!

Knowing that I was going to have to implement different habits, habits that served me and got me to the end result of dropping a hundred-plus pounds! WHAT'S THE DIFFERENCE, again!

Didn't bring me buckets of life lessons and peace. Quite the opposite. I'm standing there thinking . . .

WHEN ARE YOU GOING TO LEARN, SUSAN?

WHAT? YOU GOTTA BE HIT IN THE HEAD ONE MORE TIME?

LIKE A HUNDRED EXTRA POUNDS OF WEIGHT WASN'T ENOUGH, NOW YOU GOTTA BE A DRUNK???

LIFE LESSON NUMBER TWELVE THOUSAND, or what???

ENOUGH!

ENOUGH WITH THE GROWTH.

GIVE ME IGNORANCE, PLLLLLLLLEEEEEEASE
was how I was feeling at the time.

You wanna run the marathon of sobriety?
    You wanna win?
    You wanna be sober and stay that way?
Here are the questions you need the answer to:

Where is the motivation going to "come from"?

What's going to be different this time?

How do you expect to be able to "maintain" this
    time?

What other lifestyle habits do you need to develop
    that will be there for you, serve you, get you
    where you want to go (sober), and what do you
    need to do to change the ones that don't?

How to stay sober is what I worked on. That's all I
worked on. Everything else stopped for a while because
nothing else means anything till you are sober. Not money,
not success, not the love you may have in your life. All of
it will be clouded by your progressive, fatal disease. After
a while you really don't have much to do with your life.
Not you, the person that cares about their health, loves
their family, wants to be responsible. You have taken a
backseat in this bus ride. Until you are "stayed" stopped,
it's the addict at the wheel of your drinking bus ride from
hell . . .
    Addiction is different for every alcoholic.
    The story is different.

The end is the same.

It owns you . . .

So here's what we have to do if you don't want to be owned by your disease. If you want to live, easily, without alcohol and stop having your life lived with alcohol in control, you gotta have the plan.

The one plan with two sides, both equally important, both at the same time, side by side.

Body and mind healing. You've got to heal. The work that you are going to be doing daily, both mentally and physically is not difficult, it won't take much of your time. It will help you stay stopped drinking. If you don't do it, chances are you'll be drinking again "before you know it," like the other twelve thousand times you/I quit drinking.

Not a problem. Very formula. Very understandable.

"The beginning of quitting drinking is simply a matter of making a decision and then sticking to it by stubbornly refusing to indulge. So pick a time— like NOW and KNOCK IT OFF."

How about it? No more. No more alcohol in your life. No more destruction, it's time to rebuild. No more shame, it's time for pride. Enough with the fear, it's time for a plan that works to help you not be scared but informed.

So let's go and knock it off, shall we?

R̲ First thing that you have to do is support your body and mind in sobriety. And the physical part of the plan involves different things.

$\boxed{\text{R}_\text{x}}$ First, getting you what you need to eliminate the cravings for alcohol that your addicted brain is going to have.

If there is someone you know that is going to have a problem with that statement, just have them follow this line of thinking . . .

Your body and brain are addicted to a drug, and when you stop drinking, it's not going to have what it's addicted to anymore.

Could there be a possibility that your body would crave it???

Yes. No question about it. So getting you the biochemical balancing your body needs to heal, saturating your brain, central nervous system, liver, digestive tract—your body—with the nutrients, vitamins, and minerals that you so desperately need, that will help you maintain a foundation of recovery, stability, health, and balance, is . . . ?

ONE OF THE MOST IMPORTANT THINGS YOU CAN DO.

Remember Diagram Man, remember the physical damage. That damage must be healed and the missing vitamins . . . must be replaced!

"The biochemical makeup of the brain has been so severely altered by alcohol it has to be balanced."

There's no question that this vitamin-saturation thing seems to make a whole lot of sense, but there's a bit of a problem with the medical/recovery community when you mention the word *vitamins*.

Vitamins heal? *Don't be so ridiculous!*

Vitamins having anything to do with health? *Be quiet. Come on, up on the table . . . Let's cut it out (literally) . . .*

Vitamins able to solve the physical problem? *Stop it, you're killing me. Fill this prescription and shut up.*

I remember doing the *Home Show*—ABC, you know —just a few short years ago and having America's favorite doctors scoff at the concept that vitamins E, C, D, A, any of the B's had anything to do with anything. And just a few short years later, those same "America's favorite" doctors are in the vitamin business . . . after finding out they were wrong.

The easiest way to explain the importance of the nutrients is just to lay out what I—and my brother and thousands of others—have been taking, and its function in the body. Here's what the experts say:

Alcohol has many effects on the human body.* One of the easiest to overlook is the way it negatively influences nutritional status. There are three mechanisms by which alcohol is believed to impair nutritional status. One is that, for chronic drinkers, alcohol often replaces food, and the resulting reduction in food intake contributes to lower-than-adequate levels of all nutrients, including proteins,

---

* The information in this and the following twelve paragraphs was provided to Susan Powter by Prof. Zakir Ramazanov, Ph.D., a world-renowned researcher in plant molecular biology and the director of science for the European Institute of Applied Sciences. It is included here *as educational material only* and is not intended to be used for the sale or promotion of any products.

carbohydrates, lipids, vitamins, and minerals. Another mechanism is alcohol's ability to impair the function of the digestive tract. Alcohol inhibits the stomach and intestinal enzymes from digesting many of the foods that are eaten. In addition, it is believed that excessive consumption of alcohol impairs the absorption of nutrients through the intestinal membranes into the blood. Finally, as mentioned elsewhere in this book, alcohol is known to have significant physiological effects on the chemistry of the body. Such chemical effects are believed to prevent the proper utilization of some of the nutrients that are absorbed.

Thus, where alcohol is involved, the vital elements that the body needs to function normally have three hurdles to cross, three strikes against them, which diminish their chances of being utilized in the way nature intended. With such adverse conditions, it is no wonder that nutritional-deficiency syndromes including anemia, neurological disorders, and vitamin and mineral deficiencies are frequently seen in alcoholics. In western society, alcoholics constitute the largest group of patients with treatable nutritional deficiencies. Some of the important nutrients affected by alcohol are:

Calcium: Beyond its most notable role as the primary element in our bones, calcium is absolutely essential for almost all electrical activity in the body. Nowhere is it more important than in the brain.

Magnesium: Magnesium levels are conspicuously low among alcoholics undergoing detoxification, and magnesium deficiencies have been linked to other neurological problems. The most notorious are premenstrual syndrome and stress symptoms. Magnesium supplementation has been shown to improve liver-cell function and overall muscle strength in alcoholics, regardless of abstinence.

Zinc: This element can be viewed as a gatekeeper; it is critical for proper function of the immune system, which recognizes the difference between good substances and potentially harmful ones that must be removed from the body.

Amino acids: Amino acids are the building blocks of proteins, necessary for tissues in every organ (in fact, in every cell of the body). In "treatment," alcoholics with lower levels of amino acids are known to experience more severe symptoms, such as hallucinations and emotional problems, than those who have sufficient levels. Supplementation has been shown to improve liver function.

Essential fatty acids (EFA): Yes, certain fats are essential to good health! Such nutrients, like gamma linolenic acid (GLA), are the starting material used to make cell membranes, the most important component of the cells of the brain. EFAs have been shown to "play an important role in altering some of the deleterious effects of ethanol."

Vitamins A, C, and E: These are the antioxidant vitamins, which play a critical role in preventing free-radical damage to the cells of the body. Like a construction company, our cells use DNA as a set of blueprints to build or repair anything and everything in the body. Many chemicals, particularly alcohol, can damage these blueprints, making repair difficult, impossible, or worse—some types of DNA damage can even cause cancer. It is this very form of damage inflicted upon DNA that these vitamins are believed to be effective against. These antioxidants also protect the lipids important in brain function, mentioned in the preceding EFA section.

Other antioxidants and related nutrients: Other nutrients that are believed to be helpful in preventing free-radical damage to the body are also being studied for their effects in chronic abusers of alcohol. Most notable is the herb kudzu, which is known to supply antioxidant isoflavones. *Rhodiola rosea* (commonly known as goldenroot) appears to be a multifaceted nutrient; in addition to being a potent antioxidant, it contains sylmarin, the active ingredient in milk thistle, believed to support the healthy liver function. Furthermore, supplementation with *Rhodiola rosea* may also enhance the brain's essential neurochemicals, dopamine and serotonin. In fact, *Rhodiola rosea* extract has been used in Russian alcohol "recovery" programs and studies for many years.

Pancreatic enzymes: Enzymes are a unique group of substances that the healthy pancreas churns out in heaps. These pancreatic enzymes are responsible for breaking down the foods we eat into molecules that are small enough to be absorbed through the cells of the intestines and into the bloodstream. Unfortunately, the pancreas is damaged by alcohol consumption, but the good news is that research indicates that abstinence can restore pancreatic function. While the pancreas is recovering it may be helpful to supplement the diet with these enzymes to get the most benefit from the foods we eat.

L-glutamine: One of the many amino acids found in proteins, l-glutamine has an incredible reputation among recovering alcoholics. Many report that taken supplementally, the free form (that is, when it is alone and not part of proteins) of l-glutamine can stop the cravings for alcohol within minutes.

A NOTE ON QUALITY:

It is important to note that the above nutrients can be found in many supplemental products, which is good news for recovering alcoholics. But, consumer beware! Not all forms of these nutrients are equal. For example, calcium carbonate, otherwise known as chalk, is often used in cheaper, less expensive calcium supplements. The adage "you get what you pay for" was never more applicable. For example, research shows that it is very difficult for your body to absorb calcium carbonate into the bloodstream; most passes right through the body—in other words, much of the money spent on calcium supplements that really provide nothing more than chalk is actually being flushed right down the toilet. But when calcium and other minerals are chelated to amino acids, they can then be transported into the bloodstream far more efficiently. Chelated minerals work better because this is the form of mineral that nature intended for us to eat. A similar phenomenon is responsible for the superiority of natural vitamin C and natural beta carotene over their synthetic counterparts: In addition to poor absorption, synthetic, low-quality supplements often carry chemical residues, which may hamper the recovery effort. These are the reasons why it is imperative to use only the highest-quality, all-natural nutritional supplements from a reputable source.

I'm not gonna sit here and tell you that I even know exactly what vitamin took what urge away. That's what biochemists are for, and there's plenty of them out there. But I can very easily tell you about the difference in the way I felt when I stopped drinking with nutritional support and the way I felt without it, and the difference is night and day. One is cloaked in darkness, fear, and seemed to last forever (like all sleepless nights do), and the other is covered in possibilities, hope, and light.

Here's what was happening to me physically without any nutritional support, every time I failed. It no longer happens to me, and I've succeeded.

Here is one example of an afternoon after I'd quit drinking for good without nutritional support.

As convinced as the day is long is what I was when I was at the meeting with Rusty on this particular afternoon.

I'd been convinced that I was never going to drink again for the last three days. Sober for three days and staying that way was the way I felt about it.

She knew, I knew, we both knew that I had quit drinking.

And I had, without a problem—until I was driving up the street, at four-thirty in the afternoon, on the way home, when I said, "Rusty, I'm going to have a drink."

The talking began, the logic, the rationale, all the reasons why I didn't want to were beautifully presented to me by someone who loves me, respects me, and was trying to help me not drink. It didn't matter. Nothing mattered. Because physically I was driven. I'm telling you, *driven* is the best way to describe what I was feeling.

It wasn't an emotional problem . . . I was working sobriety, listing all the things that meant the world to me. Using the mental discipline that has helped me stay convinced and committed in so many other areas in my life.

I was working it . . . running the list in my brain.

The reasons I wanted to stand by my decision not to drink anymore.

The things in my life that would benefit from sobriety.

The truth about drinking and what it does to my life.

Running it, running it, and running it some more . . .

Telling the truth—I wasn't having a problem doing that . . . I wasn't in denial. I knew good and well I was an alcoholic and that alcohol was controlling my life.

Character defect, my ass. I'm telling you (and you know exactly what I'm talking about), nothing mattered. I had to have a drink. Nothing in the world could stop me from drinking a beer.

No logic.

No rationale.

No thinking, nothing . . . Something else was happening.

There was a physical urge that was unbelievably strong. And it took over. I was struggling. Struggling. Driven. Aching. Hurting. Incapable of focusing on anything else.

That's the truth.

\!!!/

You wanna know what nutritional support has meant to me in sobriety? All the difference in the world.

When it comes to being able to walk through the truth, think, get to my conviction, it has meant success versus failure, which means it has meant everything.

Nutritional support did that for me by eliminating the physical urge to drink, balancing my blood sugar, repairing the internal damage that I did by drinking, applying the ointment—biochemical support—rubbing the balm in the wound . . . and building the habits that gave me a real sense of feeling physically (I'm not talking energy level here for everyone reading who's just waiting to call the newspapers and tell them that the hyperactive buzz-cut fitness queen is calmer) calmer. I'm talking about a true physical balance.

The internal frenzy that was connected to the *urge* to drink is gone.

From frenzy to thought, being able to take a minute and think. That's what you are going to have the advantage of in your daily sobriety with biochemical support.

Nutritional support has calmed down the fear.

I once said to Rusty in all honesty—before nutritional support in sobriety, during one of the thousand times I quit drinking—"If this is what it feels like every day to live sober, I don't know if I can do it."

I felt bad. I don't anymore.

There was an incredible physical urge to drink that made walking through, doing the other work that's so necessary in sobriety, so much more difficult. Not anymore.

I am a functioning human being and I'm telling you the absolute truth when I tell you that fighting the urges to drink was really, really, tough and I couldn't do it successfully until I got the nutritional support that we all need to be able to do the work we have to do to stay sober . . .

I've done both, that's why I can fully understand the 12 percent recovery success rate in AA.

I tried it both ways and it's easy to see why AA doesn't even go past a year of sobriety in their stats for success.

I know why most people don't make it. It's easy, easy, easy to see why the fear of drinking again is sooo real to most of us suffering from this disease. Without any physical treatment it is very optimistic to assume that you will be able to ever stay stopped drinking.

Living without that constant urge to drink is much, much easier. It's more practical, more realistic. It's a better way to be sober.

There is no question that to feel physically balanced makes doing the other work that needs to be done possible.

I am more capable of, able to, because the nutritional support has given me something that I and you need to stay sober.

A moment.

I have a moment before the reaction to think.

I could take a moment and hear the voice (wait till you hear about the voices).

I could find a place to go to rationally make the decision that the other me's wanted to make (wait till you hear about the other me's).

Without the frenzy, without the urge, without the physical push to have a drink, there is the thought and then some time to make a logical, rational decision, without the physical drive demanding the alcohol.

The vitamin nutritional support gave me that. And in that moment I have the other tools I need to make a different decision, changing the course of my life, literally.

I didn't find some kind of magic. This information is all over the place.

Just pick up *Eating Right to Live Sober* by Katherine Ketcham and Ann Mueller.

Run out and get J. Mathews Larson's *Seven Weeks to Sobriety*.

And definitely run out and buy *Under the Influence* by James Robert Milam.

Or call me—and get the information you need for the best vitamin plan out there for sobriety . . . Do whatever you want, whatever works for you, but get it.

Get your brain, body, and soul the support it so needs and so deserves. That way you can get on with doing all the work that needs to be done for you to live, without the struggle, the urge, the ache, the pounding in your brain daily to drink, drink, drink, drink, drink, drink . . . Don't wait for "them" to understand, just do it.

There is nothing outrageous about the statement that nutritional (even though the AMA, the media, and everyone else who is interested in keeping this common-bloody-sense thinking out of your brain is going to jump all over it like flies on . . .) support, physical treatment for the disease of alcoholism, could be nothing but advantageous.

It's not difficult to understand, but having it happen in your life is not as easy as it should be. Hopefully, books like this, you and I getting educated about our disease and insisting on changes in the recovery community, will change that . . . but for now, your doctor is clueless, your local recovery community is clueless, and there isn't a life raft for miles and miles in this ocean of recovery, so it's gonna be up to you to save your own life. You must be proactive, strong, informed, and educated about your own disease and get the help you need.

NEXT in your physical sober plan? . . .

Sugar

Life Without Sugar 101.

It's a fine line I'm walking here . . . Call the circus and tell 'em you've got a new tightrope gal—me!

Here's my dilemma. This is not a food book. Done that with the *Food* book, by Susan Powter. Love that book. This is a book about drinking and not doing it anymore.

Sober and staying that way is what we are talking about, and we can't talk about staying sober without talking about food.

Sugar, to be precise. Can't talk staying sober without talking sugar. So, see my dilemma?

Probably not, because it's really not very clear, but it will be . . .

Sugar is a big problem in our disease. Because sugar and alcohol are almost one and the same (first really bad reaction, I'm sure, from any naysayer reading . . .), and sugar ain't just sugar when you are talking about alcoholism, because you can't even say the word *sugar* without saying the word *hypoglycemia*. And that's where it gets sticky, very, very sticky. It's a blood-sugar problem that, depending on who you are talking to, millions of Americans are suffering from and dealing with the horrific symptoms of . . .

depression
irritability
exhaustion
anxiety
mood swings
and
alcoholism (yep, they are connected).

You and your blood sugar. Me and my blood sugar and the balancing of it. That's what we gotta spend some time on if you want one of the best defenses you can get to support your sober life.

Balancing blood sugar is a complicated process that involves your pancreas, your brain, your endocrine glands, adrenal, pituitary, thyroid, and your digestive tract . . . and our bodies handle it quite well. Designed beautifully, this body of ours, to do its complicated work daily. This machine—can't say enough about it. These bodies that house our heart and soul—brilliant, except when we step in and screw them up.

Could you imagine what happens to that complicated, normal, "our bodies can handle it" process of balancing blood sugar when we eat 150 pounds of refined sugar a year?

A little too much, would you say—or what the average American eats?

You can double that for teenagers and probably triple it for most people . . .

One hundred and fifty pounds a year of almost anything would cause a problem, but when you are talking sugar, you have nooo clue the havoc it creates!

So far my little sugar discussion shouldn't be a problem. It's pretty simple and logical to suggest that taking in 150 pounds of sugar a year may cause . . .

side effects?
consequences?
connections to other problems?

Easy to figure that one out. Nothing too big about that statement. We eat a TON of sugar.

Balancing blood sugar is a delicate, complicated process, so maybe eating 150 pounds could throw some things off???

Well, you wouldn't think so, but here's where it gets a little tricky, because when you are talking to the AMA, AA, or any other A that has anything to do with you and me getting sober, and you bring up sugar, the enormous amount we eat a year, and anything to do with sobriety, it's considered blasphemy.

All hell breaks loose, and if you want denial . . . that's exactly what you are going to get if you ask the A's to make the sugar-and-alcohol connection.

But the fact is, there are enormous connections between your sugar intake and your sobriety. Cravings for alcohol and for sugar are as connected as Siamese twins.

It's wonderful information that is going to make your

sober living sooooo very much easier, and it's imperative we talk about it.

Let's start with the similarities.
 Refined sugar and alcohol . . . oh, how similar they are.

 both:
 simple carbohydrates

 both:
 zippo nutritional value

 both:
 completely empty and "lots of 'em" calories

 both:
 very, very fast absorbers

 both:
 cause intense cravings

 both:
 the fastest, the quickest, the best way to dump the
   glucose into your body . . . fast, fast, fast

 both:
 "sugar-rich liquids"

 A few similarities, for sure. And the differences?
 Sugar is something you need to live. Alcohol is not.
 Sugar in its natural state is essential to your body, like fat is essential to your body.
 Sugar provides energy in a form your body can use best. It's found naturally in fruits, veggies, and grains. It's important.

Sugar in its natural form has so many of its own properties to absorb, metabolize, and to digest.

Why, our bodies couldn't live without it!!! (EXCUSE ME . . . did anyone else besides me just detect a tone of Scarlett from *Gone with the Wind* in that statement? I am fully prepared for "Rhett, but Rhett, dahlin' " to come out of my mouth next . . . When did I walk down that mahogany stairway?)

Yeah, sugar is essential, just like fat is essential.

Without fat, your body couldn't insulate internal organs or regulate body temperature. . . . It's essential.

The health problems we are facing in our society today —second in the world in heart disease, morbid obesity a national epidemic, childhood obesity increased 54 percent in the last fifteen years (there's something that's gonna help our standings in the world: millions of morbidly obese, sick, no-energy-and-strength kids)—don't have anything to do with fat being some kind of horrible thing, but have everything to do with the enormous amount (43 percent of our daily caloric intake) we take in daily.

And our sugar intake? Same. It's not that sugar (in its natural state) is bad at all, it's that we are TAKING IN A TON OF IT . . .

And just like fat, there's one more thing that needs to be considered, other than the amount we take in yearly. There are big, big problems with the *kind* of sugar we are taking in.

Fat saturated, cholesterol, animal products out the wazoo . . . not so good.

Sugar refined—unbelievably damaging.

Poison versus food. Real versus fake.

Refined white sugar—I'm telling ya, you are not gonna believe this stuff . . .

Sugar as we know it today, on our table in a little dish, in small colorful packages, to be poured on, sprinkled in, and cubed wherever you need some sweetening, is a by-product. It's a non-food. There is nothing real about it.

It doesn't resemble sugar (the stuff that nature made) in any way, shape, or form. You can't consider it sugar, not after the food boys have gotten their filthy little hands on it. By the time you get what was sugar, it's been pulled, shredded; every cell has been ruptured by a hydraulic roller to release as much liquid as possible; then the liquid cane juice has been strained and boiled with lime salt, evaporated, poured into trays, where it's heated and evaporated again; then it goes through a spinning, meshing, bleaching process . . . and what's left is white sugar crystals.

Refined sugar is processed by a multiple chemical processing of the juice of the sugarcane, it removes all of the fiber and the protein which amounts to 90 percent of the plant.

What you are left with is 10 percent—a very concentrated, very powerful, zero-nutrition non-food—and if you want an explosion, you got it in this empty-calorie junk that can do some major damage. You've got a nuclear bomb.

That's what we are talking about from now on every time I say *sugar.* Not what's grown naturally.

Who doesn't love sweet?

What a fresh piece of fruit. The syrup from the tree.

The comb of the honey . . . yuuuuuuuummmmm, Pooh Bear will tell you . . .

But Pooh didn't get caught in the refined-sugar package, 'cause if he had, he'd be dead! That would be one dead bear if that's where his nose had gotten stuck . . .

You can't even talk about heart disease and diabetes without talking about the amount of and kind of sugar we are eating.

Obesity and sugar—something we've known for years . . . they're one and the same problem.

Diabetes and sugar—any connection?

Depression and sugar—so connected it isn't even funny (sorry, you probably aren't laughing if you are depressed, but you know what I mean).

Immune system weakening—refined sugar!

Cancer connected to sugar—sure, it has been.

Ulcers, sugar—very much connected (and you thought it was only stress). "Ulcers may be a sugar sickness."

Sugar can "undo your kidneys by causing edema and hypertension."

It wreaks havoc, causing enormous irregularities in your body's insulin response.

If you're interested in out-of-control hormone levels— sugar, sugar, sugar.

High blood pressure, sugar—just ask your doctor about the connection:

It's a pancreas whacker of all time . . .

Flips your brain out totally. If you don't believe me, eat half a pound of sugar . . . see how ya act.

"[White refined sugar] has been implicated in obe-sity, tooth decay, diabetes, and many psychological and emotional problems.*"*

One plus one equals two . . .

We are eating a ton of this no-nutritional-value stuff. It's been connected to alllll kinds of problems with our health. The boys at the AMA know it, and have known it for a long, long time. . . . It's been understood for years that refined white sugar is considered a "nutritional culprit in disease. It weakens our tissue health and our body resis-tance."

If you want to take your own sweet responsibility and find out more about this non-food that we are eating wayyyyyy tooo much of in our world, just go get these books, written by these fabulous people who had the chutzpah years ago to come out and tell the truth:

Sugar Blues, by William Dufty
Licking the Sugar Habit, by Nancy Appleton
The Disease Your Doctor Won't Treat, by Geraldine
    Saunders and Dr. Harvey M. Ross
Body, Mind and Sugar, by E. M. Abrahamson
The Low Blood Sugar Handbook, by Patricia and
    Edward Krimmel
Hypoglycemia: A Better Approach, by Paavo Airola

So there you have it. All the books you need to catch up on refined white sugar and what it does to our health. It's bloody interesting, but not what we are talking about . . . so read up on your own time. (Charming, very host-like, warm, welcoming???) We've got something very, very important to talk about: you, your sobriety, and sugar.

It's not going to be difficult for you to make this "massive thread in the cable" connection between sobriety and sugar, but let me warn you that it's going to be very, very tough for the boys at the AMA, your doctor, AA, and most of the people you meet.

Because the truth of the alcoholic matter is that craving alcohol after you stop drinking and sugar are sooooooo connected you won't believe it. Most alcoholics begin to crave sweet as soon as they stop drinking.

From a bottle of whiskey to a huge bowl of ice cream —it's not an exaggeration for millions of people. Have a look at any AA meeting around. What do you see? Church basement, coffee, doughnuts, and sugar, sugar, sugar, sugar . . .

"Low blood sugar causes a craving for substances such as alcohol."

"Recovering alcoholics often become sugar addicts, they crave sugar the way they once craved alcohol."

"The symptoms do not simply disappear when the alcoholic stops drinking and he [they] must therefore carefully regulate his [their] blood sugar intake to control the level of glucose in the blood."

"Before and after rehab many alcoholics crave alcohol.**"**

I've seen it with almost every recovering alcoholic I've ever met. Suzi, my friend and researcher, just bumped into a guy that everyone knows was a big drinker. He's sober, good on ya, buddy. She congratulates him, and asks him how he's feeling.

"Glad to be sober, but a little edgy. Not sleeping so well. Hanging on one day at a time."

Right. So Suzi asks the obvious question . . .

"Have you changed your diet (sugar intake) since you quit drinking?"

He says "yeah."

(Suzi thinks, *Great, he's improved it* . . .)

"I'm adding sugar to my coffee. Never did that before.

"Sugar on my sugared cereal. Never did that before.

"Started eating doughnuts. Never did that much before."

Why? Because—his words (that would be the reason for the quotes, I suppose)—"I'm really into Big Hunks." Now, my friends, you may be asking, what in the hell is a big hunk? (Seventies saying for a good-looking guy?) No, candy. A candy bar . . .

It's a big white mass of sugar and nuts . . . and this guy loves 'em.

Because he found himself getting really tired.

Found himself on edge.

And guess what helps alleviate the symptoms . . . SUGAR!

!ᵕᵕ!

Bill, the charismatic founder of AA, knew it . . . He was interested in the connection between his drinking and his "enormous" sugar intake. He was also interested in the connection (and oh what a connection there is) between his depression and his "enormous" sugar intake.

So what did he do? He got rid of sugar, "stabilized his blood sugar and achieved a sense of well-being."

Robert Meiers, M.D., from Santa Cruz, California, has studied the connection between your drinking and your sugar intake, and guess what he found out? Ninety-five percent of alcoholics studied suffered from low blood sugar.

Emanuel Cheraskin, M.D., did the low-blood-sugar test, and guess what? Between 75 and 90 percent of the alcoholics he tested had low-blood-sugar problems.

John Tinterna, M.D., endocrinologist, figured it out after years and years of study . . . Our staying sober after we stop drinking has a whole lot to do with the fact that "recovered alcoholics who have been sober for many years continue to suffer the effects of hypoglycemia."

If you think the word *vitamin* stirs up some dust, you've never seen a dust storm like the one that is stirred up every time you say the word hypoglycemia in the presence of anyone medical . . .

LOW BLOOD SUGAR

irritability
depression

aggressiveness
insomnia
fatigue
restlessness
confusion
desire to drink
nervousness

Wow, could you imagine being a sober alcoholic and one of the 95 percent of us still suffering from the symptoms of low blood sugar?

Can you imagine walking around daily feeling nervous, irritable, confused, tired? Sure you can, because without nutritional support, that's probably how you are living sober.

YUCK, what a way to live. No wonder you have to hang on one day at a time.

Up until yesterday the effects of low blood sugar, as something 95 percent of us alcoholics suffer from, was called "dry-drunk syndrome" . . . Guess what the symptoms of dry-drunk syndrome are . . .

irritability
depression
aggressiveness
insomnia
fatigue
restlessness
confusion

desire to drink
nervousness

Identical???

So Bill Wilson, Dr. Emanuel Cheraskin, Dr. John Tinterna, Dr. J. Mathews Larson, and Dr. Ann Mueller all kinda have a point? Sure they do! And so do I—a point to make that is . . . why, oh why haven't you been given this information?

Are you starting to see it? Beginning to see the possibility of some kind of connection between your blood sugar dropping to your toes, the fast-absorbing, nutritionally void, instant-energy poisons of refined sugar, and you craving another source of what, on many levels, has the exact same effect in your body—alcohol?

Glucose deprivation. Ever heard of it? Well, you live it daily if you are a recovered (or want to be) alcoholic that isn't getting the nutritional support and healing you need.

Have a look at the effects of alcohol on your body and the effects of sugar on your body, and you tell me.

Sugar causes a couple of things that alcohol cures.

It's time to think *glucose dump,* and understand what it means, so that you can connect it to your sobriety.

You eat refined white sugar. You get a rush. There is a surge of energy in your body. Your pancreas gets the message that you have a sugar overload. It starts producing insulin like you can't imagine. It overproduces (giving you one of the most oversensitive pancreases of all time) insulin. All hell is breaking loose inside your body while your pancreas is working overtime doing the job it needs to do so you can still stand up and function because of the insulin overload that the nuclear bomb that you've just eaten is creating.

You've whacked it out by dumping way too much of this concentrated (never meant to be eaten in this state, remember) bleached white junk into your body and . . .?

You get the sugar high. For a while.

Then—another one of life's little universal principles happens—the low.

Happens every time . . .

What goes up has got to go down . . .

And down you are gonna go when it comes to refined white sugar . . .

sluggish
not so sharp
tired
cranky

You don't feel good. A low doesn't feel good, but a high does.

Your body is trying desperately to balance, because balance is right, balance is what your body needs. Guess what can do the job really quickly? The balancer of all time when it comes to glucose and your body . . .?

Guess what can make that low feel instantly better than you could ever imagine feeling?

"[When you eat a ton of sugar and cause a glucose imbalance,] you cause a craving for alcohol or sweets."

Sugar and . . . ???

Alcohol.

They both give you that quick glucose lift . . . the high to the low.

Both alcohol and sugar relieve the symptoms of low blood sugar.

The yin to the yang.

The swing to the pendulum.

They both make you feel better immediately.

Now, not feeling so good isn't so bad (another statement you might have to reread to understand the sense of).

Flu, you don't feel so good.

Cold, can't sleep, sore thumb, whatever . . . You don't feel good.

You could try an aspirin and see if that makes you feel any better. If it gets worse you could go to the doctor in a couple of days. Tired? You could go to bed early tonight and see how you feel tomorrow . . . That's not feeling so good.

Craving and not feeling so good, states that 90 percent of us live with the minute we stop drinking, is a whole other story . . . Let's talk *craving,* shall we?

Look it up:

Crave; craving: to long for eagerly, desire strongly . . . an intense or prolonged desire, yearning, appetite . . .

Yearn?

Yearn for something? What does that mean? Can you yearn and be completely clear and balanced, able to make good decisions?

Not once you know the meaning of the word:

Yearning: deep or anxious longing.

When you are "fighting an urge to drink," is it a casual thought in the middle of the day, just a twinge, a mild-headache kind of feeling that an aspirin could cure?

Is that voice in your brain suggesting the drink just a mild whisper or one hell of a strong voice? Which one is it?

Are you hearing, *Hey, maybe I'll have a nice cold beer this afternoon,* or are you physiologically in deep and anxious longing?

Are you living with an intense and prolonged desire to balance something? More like an incredible urge?

Anything in order to feel better? *Something* has gotta be done to stop all the symptoms? Ready to do *whatever* it takes???

And if so, what could you do to instantly stop it?

DRINK.

Instantly fix the glucose problem going on in your body and your mind. Drinking does that.

I know that I've written the "You aren't a weak-willed weenie" to death. You and I and anybody else reading this knows that our behavior comes with the disease. No "characteristics of an alcoholic," not anymore, in our thinking, yep, yep, yep . . . But now you are about to find out why. Why our behavior is affected. Why it is as inevitable as the rolls on the stomach.

Because the brain relies almost exclusively on glucose.

Your Brain

The brain? Important organ? Have anything to do with behavior?

"During temporary shortages of glucose the brain suffers mightily."

The urge to drink and the connection to glucose shows up when you try to stop drinking, and your body is suffering horribly. Your pancreas is desperately trying to balance, and to top it off, your brain is suffering mightily. Things are not looking good right now. It would be easy to see, in this environment, how behavior could get skewed, don't ya think? No matter how logical, no matter how responsible, no matter how much you love everyone you love.

Do you think it's really such a stretch to suggest, with all this stuff going on around some major organs in your body, that it could affect your behavior?

And since we are going out on the edge, let's just jump right off to something else that seems to be difficult for current recovery thinking, your doctor, your counselor, and anyone else connected to you, your alcoholism, and your sobriety . . .

Do you think, after getting the glucose facts, that it is reasonable to say that your commitment to stay stopped drinking could easily and completely disappear when your mind and body are in trauma? *Crisis:* dealing with an urgency. Glucose deprived. Brain dump. Pancreas dump. Everything dumping—including your big commitment to be a sober alcoholic?

YES. Of course it's connected!

Your organs are screaming for balance and that overrides your greatest intentions.

It's not about thinking things through and/or being cognitive when you are in a low-blood-sugar physiological panic. It is a matter of survival. You haven't failed thousands of times because you have a character defect. How about the concept that you weren't getting treatment for your glucose-deprived brain, your low-blood-sugar state, your severely imbalanced body? . . .

When the brain is deprived of the fuel that it needs to function—glucose—"it registers its complaints in the form of headaches, confusion, irritability, nervousness, or depression." Low blood sugar seems to be very connected to how you are feeling, the energy your brain has or doesn't have, and a craving for something else that will do the same thing—alcohol?

And hypoglycemia and low blood sugar? Same thing?

When it comes to hypoglycemia there is fighting going on around the word, the meaning, how to figure it out, who's suffering, what it does, and how severe it is.

The boys in the AMA believe that very few, if any, people suffer from hypogylcemia. And the other school of thought, everybody else under the sun's thought, is that millions of people are suffering with, dying from, and hurting real, real bad because of low blood-sugar levels.

"Hypoglycemia is not a widespread phenomenon, contrary to much of the press devoted to it in recent years."

"Many people claim to suffer from low blood sugar, or hypoglycemia and blame it for their fatigue, drowsiness, or anxiety, but true hypoglycemia is rare."

215

Let's talk about what low blood sugar means.

We all know it's not a good thing to have big highs and lows going on in your body when it comes to your blood-sugar levels. Even the AMA knows that.

The problem with hypoglycemia is in the AMA's or your local doctor's ability to interpret whether or not that is happening in your body.

You see, they have a different interpretation than every other health professional out there . . . they interpret the test everyone uses differently.

And the test that the boys can't seem to interpret correctly is . . . the glucose tolerance test.

Standard hypoglycemia testing. Here's how it's done:

No food or stimulants after ten at night.
Next morning, blood test.
And it's recorded.
Then the patient drinks a ton of quick-energy sugar.
Right after that, more blood is taken.
Another half hour, more blood.
And then hourly for a total of five to six hours.

It is designed to show how the blood-sugar level in your body responds to a concentrated dose of glucose. That's the point. Everyone agrees on that. . . . It's the *number* that they are having big, big fights over and can't seem to come to any understanding or agreement on (years after the test was developed). The number that means you actually are hypoglycemic. That's the problem.

• • •

Some physicians are not concerned unless the blood sugar drops below fifty milligrams percent. Others argue that no abnormality exists unless the blood sugar falls below fifty milligrams percent and the patient experiences symptoms at the lowest point. Some other doctors, though, the experts, read these tests with a more sensitive eye, and they consider a ten-point fall from the beginning of the first blood sample hypoglycemia.

So . . . the *experts* are watching things like how fast your blood sugar is falling.

The doctors are staring at the fifty-milligram point.

The speed of the drop is considered most important by the real *experts*.

The doctors are staring at the fifty-milligram point.

The real experts question the patient's symptoms during the drop.

The doctors are staring at the fifty-milligram point.

The experts are looking at symptoms like exhaustion, depression, insomnia, and headache, and including those symptoms in their diagnosis.

The doctors are staring at the fifty-milligram point.

The experts understand that an inability to stay stopped drinking could, in fact, have a whole lot to do with low blood sugar.

The doctors are staring at the fifty-milligram point.

The experts are asking questions like:

"How are you feeling?"

"What effects does the blood-sugar drop seem to be having on your behavior?"

"How is your body managing it?"

It's called whole . . . holistic . . . a much, much bigger word (in more ways than you could ever imagine) than the three letters *AMA.*

Because the AMA can't seem to find their definition, place of diagnosis, or reason to call it a disease. They consider it rare, and rarely consider it at all. While everyone else in the field believes that up to 20 million people in this country are suffering from it.

Hypoglycemia is not a problem for you unless you are one of the 20 million that might be suffering when your doctor says you aren't, or unless you are alcoholic.

"In 1981 a survey conducted by Dr. Ann Mueller, said 93 percent of alcoholics tested showed disturbances in blood sugar regulation when given a five or six hour glucose tolerance test."

NOT GOOD. A VERY HIGH PERCENTAGE OF AL-COHOLICS SEEEEEEEM TO HAVE SOMETHING IN COMMON . . .

But here's the problem when you start talking about alcoholics and a blood-sugar problem. The word *hypoglycemia* pops up, all hell breaks loose, and everyone goes off on the "Hypoglycemia—is it or isn't it a real disorder?" discussion while the doctors stare at the fifty-milligram point. And . . . the discussion or consideration of whether or not our (the alcoholics') blood-sugar problems are in any way connected to our craving and desire to drink gets lost in the big hypoglycemia argument and we never get anywhere . . .

So I say let's get on with solving the problem. There's no way anyone can argue with the connection . . .

And there is no way on earth anyone can argue with the fact that there may be a few (one or two, ha, ha) problems connected with the AMAZING AMOUNT OF REFINED WHITE POISON that we are taking in . . . Just can't seem to get away from that little universal principle, can we?

Consequences of our actions. Bummer!

So we've talked about the AMA's connection.

How about AA?

How about we talk about the church basements full of caffeine and nicotine and . . .? What's the next thing that everyone recovering from alcohol you know eats a ton of?

Sugar, sugar, sugar, sugar, sugar, sugar . . .

Everybody knows it, everybody talks about it, but nobody has made the connection? How odd. A couple of steps (pardon the pun) missing???

The alcoholic-and-tons-of-sugar connection . . . let's make it if the A's can't or won't. You ready?

"Recovering alcoholics often become sugar addicts. They crave sugar the way they once craved alcohol."

"From an ice cream cone to a bottle of whiskey. Three years ago that wouldn't have sounded nuts to me. When I didn't drink I would eat three quarts of ice cream a night. Two kilos of chocolate a day . . .

> If I couldn't drink I would eat sugar, ice cream, choc-
> olate, anything. I knew I could stop, but I was one
> ornery son of a bitch, one chocolate-eating mother.
> And the end result I always ended up drinking."
>
> A Recovered Alcoholic

OK, fine, who really cares? So we crave sugar. Separate problem that we'll just deal with when it comes up? Is that your thinking? It was mine until I found out that my eating a ton of sugar had everything in the world to do with me drinking again or staying sober. And whether I stayed stopped drinking had oh so very much to do with making the sugar-and-craving connection.

!"!!

I've got another way of looking at falling off the wagon otherwise known as failing. If you just can't seem to stay committed and have an apparent lack of self-discipline and you are fatigued, cranky, imbalanced . . .

Maybe the solution is just to get balanced. Stop the glucose dumping. Make sure that brain o' yours doesn't end up in glucose deprivation, isn't so irritable, has energy that lasts and supports you in your life to get on with the work that is ahead of you, me, and every other addict trying to stay unaddicted . . . How ya gonna do it if you are walking around totally whacked out?

So you wanna get balanced. Fine, it's not difficult.

CUTTING BACK ON SUGAR 101

Cutting back on sugar sounds simple enough. Just cut back. But when you are talking about 150 pounds of anything, it would be an issue to cut it out. If you want well advertised, could you get any more well promoted than sugary sweet? Comfort? Feel-good food? Gets ya that buzz? It's a tough one to cut back, let alone eliminate. But you are going to be able to cut back, get rid of, solve the problem without so much as a glimpse of pain . . . because we are here to make it easy for ya.

Let's start by knowing that half the damage is better than the full impact.

R̥ Cut your sugar in half. If you normally put eight packets of the white stuff on your cereal, put four.

Better yet, put two.

R̥ If your daily soda intake is as ridiculous as that of most alcoholics I've ever met, cut it way, way, way back . . . a glass of water or two never hurt.

R̥ Eat half the candy bar??? OK, OK, I've gone too far, because nobody eats a half a candy bar. Maybe you won't do that, but leave the sugar out of the tea.

R̥ Breakfast cereals . . . there are some that could wipe out a town with the glucose explosion, and there are some that have no sugar. Make a better choice.

I'm gonna read you a label and you'll see what I'm talking about.

Peanut Butter Granola Bars

INGREDIENTS: GRANOLA (ROLLED WHOLE WHEAT, *SUGAR,* PARTIALLY HYDROGENATED SOY-BEAN AND/OR COTTONSEED OIL, SKIM MILK, *HONEY*), *SUGAR, CORN SYRUP,* ENRICHED WHEAT FLOUR (CONTAINS NIACIN, REDUCED IRON, THIA-MINE MONONITRATE (VITAMIN B$_1$), RIBOFLAVIN (VITAMIN B$_2$)), *INVERT SUGAR,* VEGETABLE SHORT-ENING (PARTIALLY HYDROGENATED SOYBEAN AND COTTONSEED OILS), RICE FLOUR, *CORN SYRUP SOLIDS,* PEANUT FLAVORED DROPS, *SUGAR,* PARTIALLY HYDROGENATED SOYBEAN AND COT-TONSEED OIL, PARTIALLY DEFATTED PEANUT FLOUR, SKIM MILK, SOY LECITHIN (EMULSIFIER), SALT, ARTIFICIAL FLAVOR, ROLLED OATS, GLYC-ERIN, SALT, NATURAL AND ARTIFICIAL FLAVOR, *MALT SYRUP, HIGH FRUCTOSE CORN SYRUP,* EGGS, LEAVENING (BAKING SODA, CALCIUM PHOS-PHATE), BHA (TO PRESERVE FRESHNESS), CITRIC ACID.

Check it out—different sugars.

One good way to cut back on your sugar intake is to read the labels and make the choices.

How do we cut down or stop eating the stuff that is so very much connected to us living in an agitated state of sobriety; hanging on one day at a time, white-knuckling our way through? And live a better managed, nutritionally supported (dealing with the symptoms that 95 percent of us seem to be suffering from), easier sober life?

You can do the Suzi and Susan gradual way, which would be:

Use your common bloody sense and start reading labels and doing what I've just suggested . . .

Cutting back.

Cut back so you don't feel overwhelmed. Cut back so your taste buds gradually change from totally distorted (you should hear what this stuff does to what was a normal taste) to normal. Cut back and have a look at how much better you feel. How much more energy you have. Remember you are not just getting the high with that sugar intake, you're getting the low, and your body has been working overtime. That's exhausting . . . When you stop requiring your body to do that, check out the energy you'll have. We are about to do the best cutback-on-sugar job you could ever imagine. But first you gotta know what you are taking in, and that means being able to recognize all the names of sugar:

    white refined sugar
    brown sugar
    raw sugar
    turbinado sugar
    corn syrup
    fructose
    galactose
    glucose
    fruit-juice concentrate
    honey
    lactose

maltose

maple syrup

molasses

sucrose

malt syrup

barley-malt syrup

brown-rice syrup

date sugar

sorghum

Sucanat

corn sweetener

dextrose

grape sugar

high-fructose corn syrup

invert sugar

Mannitol

Sorbital

cane sugar

SUGAR!

Cutting Back and Common Bloody Sense

If you don't think making a different choice in what you eat, can make a difference? Check this out:

Sweet	*Amount of Sugar*
glazed doughnut	6 teaspoons
plain doughnut	3 teaspoons
chocolate bar	2½ teaspoons
piece of gum	½ teaspoon

chocolate cake, one piece	10 teaspoons
brownie	3 teaspoons
cola	4 teaspoons
sparkling mineral water	0
Frosted Mini-Wheats cereal	20 grams
Grape-Nuts cereal	7 grams
cherry pie	10 teaspoons (How do you think they get those sour things to taste sweet?)
cheesecake	2 teaspoons

From ten teaspoons of sugar to one teaspoon doesn't make a difference? This is one little snacky thing we're talking here. You add up a whole day of sugar eating. You think about what not eating fifteen to twenty teaspoons a day of this refined white explosive junk will do. Difference in how you're feeling? Yes!

No question about it.

Difficult to do? YES.

It is difficult to cut back on sugar because it tastes good, especially after your taste buds have been so severely distorted by it for years.

I couldn't stand it when health-food people would suggest that an apple is as good as a frozen Snickers bar. It wasn't then, but it is now.

It is now because when I taste a Snickers bar for what it is, a cardboard, sugary concoction . . . it doesn't taste good.

An apple is better than a candy bar to me now because

I know that if I eat a candy bar I'll be walking around in a crisis for alcohol. And living in crisis doesn't feel good. I know the difference between glucose sobriety hell and being balanced and well and living sober, and no candy bar is worth craving hell.

An apple is good to me now. It's a sweet snack. If I want something a little sweeter I bake them.

You want sweet? Eat this!

ᴵᵗᵗᵗ *Suzi's Baked Apples*

Slice up 5 or 6 medium-size apples and place them in a slightly oiled 9-inch pie plate.
Pour ¼ cup apple juice over apples.
Combine in a separate bowl and stir up well:

1 *cup quick or flaked oats*
¼ *cup ground walnuts or pecans*
¼ *cup whole-wheat pastry flour*
¾ *teaspoon cinnamon*
⅓ *cup apple juice or cider*
2 *tablespoons maple syrup or honey*

Sprinkle this mixture over the apples and bake uncovered in a 350-degree oven for about 30 minutes, or until the crumbs start to brown.

SERVES EIGHT.

A Suzi cut-back-on-sugar suggestion is, eat a good meal. Now, this may sound nuts to everybody reading this, but think about it. It's really brilliance in the guise of simplicity.

If you don't want to disturb your biochemistry quite so much—your brain, your pancreas, your liver—eat a big high-volume, low-fat, high-quality meal and then have something sweet.

Suzi says, "Chances are you will want less. If you're full you are probably going to desire less (I've been saying that for the last ten low-fat years), and when you do eat some refined sugar you've already got some good, healthy food in your gut that will balance the effect of the concentrated sweet." Have you ever??? This woman is so smart. No wonder she has the most wonderful children, marriage, life you could ever imagine! Go, Suzi, go.

Yes, yes, yes, it makes a difference when you eat the fruit as opposed to the concentrated, bleached, white crap. You get the sugar, you get the fiber, and you get the vitamins.

That's how you cut down, and that may work for some of you. But a whole lot of you are gonna have to do a bit more than that.

There's a lot of people reading this book that are going to need a glucose tolerance test. Get one.

There are a lot of people reading this book who are going to have to give up refined sugar completely. Gone, forever . . . because of the damage that may have already been done, or extreme sensitivity to sugar, or you just gotta get sober now and stay that way or you'll lose everything . . .

That means

all sweets
candy
pastries

cookies
sodas
ice cream
cake
pies
cereals covered in the stuff
fruit juices

Gone, but don't worry because you'll have something better than sugar in your life. You'll have sobriety.

White Flour

The next step in your sobriety nutritional plan is to eliminate white flour.

What do you think when you think *flour?*

Old woman kneading the bread.
Essence of baking.
Grows from the earth.
Staple food.
Since the beginning of time . . . flour!
Warm.
Soft.
Smells good.
Dougheeeeeeeeeeeeee.
Fluffy flour.

That's what was. Before there were food conglomerates. Before they designed something that lives forever on your supermarket shelf. Before fast foods. Before manufacturing the cheapest possible . . . Before things had to be whiter than white.

Now when you think of flour, you gotta think

pizza dough
donuts
pretzels
pastries
bagels
waffles
pancakes

Flour. The bottom line to a whole lot of foods we eat.

Let's go back a bit, back to the old woman in her kitchen, and learn a little about how she got her flour, shall we?

The whole food that was grown from the ground was harvested and milled. That wheat berry (the original food) was/is loaded with vitamins, minerals, and fiber . . .

The old lady (sounds like a barroom marital discussion) ground the harvested berry with a big object and some kind of bowl (what do you want, culinary history? I'm writing alcoholism here) into flour, which she used for pita, if the old woman was living in India, or fortune cookies, if in fact she was a Chinese old woman. Crumpets would be the English old lady, chicken pot pie for the Aussie old lady . . . matzo bri if she was kosher.

There it is, flour as it was . . . considered the "staff of life." Farmer gal grinding and milling her staff of life to bake, to thicken, or chalk . . . Whatever she needed, the flour was there.

That was flour then. You wanna know what you are eating today?

Nothing. You are eating nothing. Paste. Play-Doh without the fun accessories. The big food companies have done it again. This time they've done the amazing. You aren't gonna believe what's been done to our staff of life . . .

Sure, it's been milled. Flour's gotta be milled, that's not the amazing part. It's how they mill and why they mill the way they mill that's gonna stump you once you know.

The berry reapers take the wheat berry and remove the bran and the germ. The germ (that's not a dirty germ, that's the outer layer of the bran) and bran are loaded with —that's loaded (pardon the drinking pun) with—vitamins, minerals, and fiber, fiber, fiber.

They remove the food in the food and then they toss it.

The bran.

The food.

The germ layer of the grain.

Which holds 83 percent of the nutrients of the little berry. The wheat berry. The stuff that flour is born with . . . Eighty-three percent of the nutrients of our staff of life is . . . ?

Dumped.

They dump it.

Throw it away.

Toss it.

Get rid of it.

Get rid of 83 percent of the value of the food . . . so?

What are you left with?

A food with very little value? Close, but not quite. You are left with a non-food with almost none of its original value and a whole lot of other stuff, dangerous stuff, added by the time they are finished.

White flour, the nineties version of the staff of life is chemically treated, bleached, whitened, and preserved. . . .

I got ya doughnut.

Ya pastry.

And ya pizza dough.

They dump the most important part of what was food for two reasons.

One, to make sure that it looks pretty.

White is pretty.

White is virginal.

White is bridal.

White is perfect . . . Every culture, ethnic group, and anything other than pure white is (and should be) throughly offended right now, but the fact is . . . when it comes to things being manufactured and presented to the public, white is still considered all those things! Sad— needs to change—but true.

And the second reason that they dump everything is so that the flour can live forever. White bleached processed flour can last for longer than you can imagine on a shelf without going bad. Good for the company manufacturing it. Good for you?

You see, when you put real food on the shelf, it can go bad, because there is something to go bad—real food. But the incredibly preserved, chemically treated, and

LOADED WITH PESTICIDES food that is called white refined flour ain't gonna go bad anytime soon because it can't support life . . . How's that for a statement?

Isn't it interesting? Yeah, probably if you are studying to be a pastry chef and want the truth about refined versus real flour . . . but what in hell does it have to do with you and your drinking?

Refined. Didn't ya see the word *refined*?

Remember *refined* and sugar?

Refined and useless?

Refined and non-food?

Refined white flour has everything, everything, everything to do with you drinking or you not drinking . . .

Sugar in its natural state—nothing wrong with it, right? It ain't gonna be the nuclear bomb that refined white sugar is, right?

Well, refined white flour—same!

Same.

Very same.

Real flour is loaded (again with the drinking pun) with nutrients and fiber. It's sweet, full of flavor, and is a food that your body can metabolize, utilize—in fact, it's one of nature's best foods.

Complex carb . . . you've heard it, unless you spend your time listening to the idiot protein boys . . . You've heard the term *complex carbohydrate.*

Our bodies can't live without carbohydrates, and the complex kind is the slower-to-digest, more-complex food that is absorbed, used, metabolized, and is a chief source of energy for our bodies . . . So, high quality would be

good, considering how important a fuel it is. And flour is
. . . in its natural state.

But after the food boys get their grubby hands all over
it???

No different from refined sugar as far as the . . .

glucose dump
explosion of energy up and the fast drop down
depression
irritability
exhaustion
anxiety
mood swings
and
urges to drink

Why?

Come on, don't lose me now. You know the answer . . .
Glucose dump, you're hurting bad. What's the best way to
feel better than better?

More glucose. Refined white flour gives us the same
glucose rush that sugar and alcohol do. I'll be damned.
Who knew? Well, a lot of people connected to the "recovery community," but not you and I till now . . . Who knew
what we were doing every time we were downing all that
dough!

Put it together.

Because it's refined and useless, it breaks down really
quickly. The food boys have taken a complex carb and
turned it into a simple nothing non-food that dumps in

fast and stresses your whole system out, just like refined white sugar.

It's concentrated. It's nutritionally void. It's a fast absorber. And it creates the swings high and low, and your body will be demanding more . . . creating an enormous imbalance. And it doesn't end there, folks. This pretty, silky, whiter-than-white flour leaves you nutritionally deficient and hankering for alcohol.

It's time we start putting together the cause and effect when it comes to the one-hundred-year-long shelf life of, the pummeling of, the destruction of the original food that is going on everywhere we look these days. It does affect our health, no matter how well advertised these enriched, tasty, good-for-ya foods say they are. There's no question anymore that these non-foods affect the way we look and feel.

Tons of refined white sugar and refined white flour does not a healthy person make.

And it's been known for a long, long time that eating white, refined, bleached junk (otherwise known as flour) is directly connected to you, your drinking, and your sobriety.

It's called a buildup to drinking. Returning to drinking. Falling off the wagon. Giving in to the urge. And it has everything to do with your physiology, not your psychology! . . .

Refined white flour contributes to it in a big, big way.

Low blood sugar causes cravings for alcohol. Refined white flour contributes to low blood sugar.

A glucose dump equals low blood sugar. Guess what creates a glucose dump. Refined, white, non-food flour.

Foods that create symptoms of depression, anxiety, confusion, exhaustion do what? Contribute to you not being able to, committed to, sticking to, confirmed and confident in sobriety? . . . !!!

These foods contribute to the decline of your health, your commitment, your ability to get and stay sober in every way! That's a fact, recovery world. When are you gonna wake up and smell the whole-grain bread!!!

OK, OK, OK . . . Even if your doctor has his/her finger up their nose when you mention anything connected to white flour and sobriety, even though when you go to the meeting the first thing you are offered is . . .

Doughnut . . .

Something sweet with your coffee and ciggy???

Go figure that one out! You, without your nutritional degree, are beginning to put this stuff together, aren't you? It's making sense, isn't it? And now what? Once you know, it's hard to act like you don't. Ignorance is better as long as you stay ignorant, but you can't. Because you want to get and stay sober, and if you do, you gotta know this.

White flour is something you might want to consider cutting back or giving up altogether . . . So? What do you do? What is this stuff being baked into?

I got the answer for ya . . . White flour is in EVERY-THING . . .

crackers
cookies
cakes
pies
pastries

breads, breads, breads, and breads
pasta
waffles
pancakes
McEVERYTHING

It's everywhere. So me sitting here suggesting that you give up flour so that you aren't walking around dying for a shot of "whatever your pleasure" seems, at this moment, to be STUPID AS HELL.

I get that. I can completely understand how you'd be thinking that, but it's not as stupid as it sounds. In fact, it's quite simple and is one of the best things you can do if you want to cut back on craving what you don't want to drink anymore.

There is flour—and there is flour (and plenty made from it) that isn't a craving, glucose disaster.

Whole grain is a flour that hasn't been raped. You can, and there are plenty of food companies that do, use whole grain to make bread. They mill it properly: they grind it into flour without throwing out anything, without stripping it useless, without bleaching it, without adding a hundred chemicals, and without making it a non-food. And they make bread out of it.

Cookies are also made out of it. How about oatmeal cookies made with oat flour (sounds reasonable), not bleached white? I've got some in my pantry right now!

Crackers and dip, not a problem . . . rye crackers (made with rye flour), rice crackers (made with rice flour), whole wheat (made with whole wheat flour) . . . See, it can be done. It's called quality versus crap.

You've heard the universal principle *Put crap in, get*

crap out—or was that someone in New Jersey who told me that? Anyway, you get the drift.

Whole-grain bagels are quite possible.

Hamburgers can still be had . . . whole-wheat buns.

Hot-dog buns, absolutely.

Waffles, pancakes . . . multigrain.

Pot pies, pastas . . . unbleached white, corn, wheat . . .

Come on, there's nothing difficult about this, and if you are willing to replace bleached white junk flour with whole grain, you get the added bonus of supporting your body in sobriety.

That's how you can do it right from the fridge or the pantry. But there's more to life than what's in your cupboard. Tell that to Old Mother Hubbard.

What about eating out?

℞ You love your Mexican food. So do I. Corn tortillas versus the bleached white flour version is a good idea if you don't want a massive glucose dump (sounds a little bathroomy, but you get it, don't ya?).

℞ Corn bread instead of white dinner rolls.

℞ Skip the bread basket and get an extra baked potato.

℞ Skip the cobbler (do two at once: refined sugar and white flour gone) and ask for a triple fruit plate.

℞ Eat one slice of pizza instead of three and get a bowl of soup to go along with it. (Yeah, and a lot of pizza parlors I've hung out in serve soup.)

℞ Eat the burger without the white flour bun . . . the old diet days, born again.

℞ Skip the bread sticks and order a plate of fresh veggies and dip.

℞ Forget about the pancakes in the pancake house (unless of course you are in a high-class joint that has multigrain pancakes) and get yourself a huge egg-white veggie omelet with extra whatever you want.

See, it isn't difficult to cut back on or eliminate this white-flour dump that is working against our sobriety.

The confusion, the complications, the "Should we or shouldn't we?" . . . the HDL, LDL, cholesterol, sugar, chemicals, organic discussion that never ends when you are talking about the food we eat . . . The complications that keep us stuck in not doing anything because we don't have a clue what to do are the real problem. The food companies want you confused because they want you to buy their product. They tell you "enriched" and you think it's better than the original. But the truth is, they've destroyed the original and have to enrich it because there's nothing left. It's hard to fight or logic your way out of the maze of the million-dollar advertising that has us all believing that it's better once it's been processed, bleached, waxed, colored, and preserved. It isn't easy to get to the truth when we are being brainwashed into believing that it has been done so much better for us.

Simple fact.

White flour bleached and processed to death is very damaging to our bodies.

It's total junk.

It's a non-food that wreaks havoc in your body.

It is directly connected to craving alcohol for alcoholics.

It does the same thing refined white sugar does.

It creates a craving (urgency, immediate, gotta have now to relieve the symptoms) for alcohol—and is very, very simple to eliminate or cut way, way, way back on, so why wouldn't ya?

Don't worry about whether or not it is environmentally safe, has been respectful to the dolphins, uses animal testing or not, or whether it's a balance in the universal scheme of things . . . just know that this stuff works against your sobriety. When you take responsibility for what you are putting into your mouth, which directly affects your body and brain, you begin to do the best thing ya ever did—stay sober.

Two minor lifestyle changes that can make a huge change in your sobriety: Not too much to ask and not too much to do.

Now there's just one more thing:

Caffeine

Caffeine.

Coffee.

Java.

The largest legal drug franchise in our country. Coffeehouses very big these days. Consider that 400 million cups of coffee a day are going down the throats of America.

Latte, frappe, sippee, dippeeeeeee, coffeeeeeeee. Couldn't be any more fashionable!

And you can count me in, I'm there. I bring my own soy milk of course, (how Beverly, how Hills of me), sucking down the java in the morning at my local coffee haus . . .

Coffee is America's number-one reason to stop what you are doing and take a break . . .

Bad news? Cup of coffee.

Tired? Cup of coffee.

Get-together? Cup of coffee.

Church gathering? Coffee!

AA meeting? Coffee, coffee, coffee . . .

Coffee is

the pot brewing
the coming together
the welcome mat for millions of people

Sit down to relax over a cup? No, truth is we are sitting down to get pumped up over a cup of America's number one drug. The number one drug in the country. More addictive—with more people addicted to—than alcohol, tobacco, and marijuana combined.

But what it represents to most of it is "the last drop," since most of us can remember:

Ahhh . . .
the smell
the warmth
the way to wake up
the first thing you do every day

Where isn't the pot brewing?

Do you have a clue how it affects you, us, our lives . . . and have you ever thought about connecting it with sobriety?

In order to understand the drug caffeine, we must for a moment go beyond the Norman Rockwell version of the pot brewing and get down to caffeine and what it really is. A drug. A strong drug. An addictive drug.

The FDA said it a long time ago . . . caffeine is a powerful central-nervous-system drug.

It's a stimulant and a diuretic.

Pain relievers = caffeine!

Your pharmacist knows that two hundred milligrams, the standard prescription dose of caffeine, is a strong drug.

He/she also knows that ten thousand milligrams of caffeine will kill ya.

So the Coffee Hut truth of the matter is . . . we are sitting down to catch a buzz with our favorite drug.

Every time we have a cup, we are getting a 150-milligram infusion of that drug.

And when you are talking about a 150-milligram shot, that's the old, canned, weak, bad version of coffee. There's much, much more caffeine in the new, stylish, double-double-mocha hocka that I just sucked down this morning (with low-fat soy, please). It's much stronger now that it's being whipped, poured over crushed ice, concentrated (how about that double espresso number that ya love?). Coffee in the nineties is being celebrated. It's tripled, it's java to the nines, it's more than a drink. The coffeehouses that are springing up on every corner are better than the bar scene ever was. It's the only place to study. It's cyberspace and a cup of . . . coffee, and it's about your sobriety.

In order to get to the bottom of the pot, we have to stop and take a moment for a little coffee history.

Before the cappuccino machine, there were a bunch of goats and their shepherd.

The shepherds of yesteryear, whenever shepherds were roaming the earth, sometime A.D.—noticed that after their goats nibbled on coffee berries, they sat down and chatted . . .

No, they got rambunctious and frisky, and you know what they say . . . nothing like a frisky goat!

Well, guess what the shepherds did. They tried a few of those frisky goat berries and got the same buzz . . . What happened between the goats and the shepherds after everyone was high as a kite is not something I think we should pursue, but the coffee buzz was discovered.

Eventually somebody opened the berry, took out the bean, and roasted it and brewed it (then Maxwell House stole the idea?), and coffee production was alive and well.

It's a good thing to produce. An addictive drug. God knows it's easy to create an audience. Just ask the alcohol boys.

Highly advertised.

Needed. Addictive.

A part of the American dream . . . as ingrained as you get!

And you? Are you addicted to coffee?

You don't need an "Are you addicted to coffee?" test

in the back of your favorite mag to find out whether you are one of millions addicted. All you and I need to confirm your drug addiction to coffee is—a day without it. Twenty-four hours with no java—and watch out!

Get ready.

Because within twenty-four hours you, me, and millions will experience the worst damn headache you've ever felt!

Vascular (caffeine constricts the small arteries in your head, hello . . .), throbbing, pounding headache beyond belief.

Gooooood, it hurts.

That's the beginning of caffeine withdrawal.

Then comes the irritability, being so annoyed and anxious, then comes the "no energy because my adrenal glands don't function on their own anymore" blues. Tired, tired, tired for days . . .

Caffeine withdrawal can last up to four days or go on for weeks. Every symptom can be immediately wiped out by doing one thing, sucking down the bean, taking a break, brewing it up, and drinking it.

So there you have it. We get addicted to an addictive drug . . .

And here's what happens when you sip it and what it has to do with you and alcohol.

You drink coffee. Your adrenal glands release an adrenal-like substance called catecholamine. (Let's break that down: cat-a-col-a-mine.)

The "cat" causes your heart to pump harder and your liver to release stored sugars.

Blood sugar rises immediately. (Are you close to seeing where we are, again, going with sobriety and blood sugar?)

Your body responds by preparing insulin in the pancreas (there's that damn pancreas working overtime again) to bring the elevated blood sugar down to normal, and you've got an overload again. An overload of insulin being produced and an overload of sugar in the bloodstream.

All that's fine and dandy for most—but let's make a very important alcoholic-hypoglycemic connection here, shall we?

Your body overproduces insulin to counteract the effects of the caffeine. It's not just normalizing, getting you back to what is balanced and right in your body, it's the overproduction of insulin that sends you into a hypoglycemic state that we are talking about.

Way, way-too-low-blood-sugar. Your body trying-to-get-it-back-to-normal and the swinging from-one-side-to-the-other-side caffeine reality for alcoholics. The balance, the blood-sugar balance takes hours to get right again. What we are talking about are the symptoms (hypoglycemic state) that you are walking around living in and the hours it takes to correct them. Hours of imbalance:

Which means urges.

Which means depression.

Which means not a lot of energy.

Anxiety?

Not a lot of strength to do the sobriety work that needs to be done. Easier to break a conviction when you are sick and tired? I think so, don't you?

And who'd a thunk that any of this could be happening over a cup of coffee?

The answer is:

Everybody.

The AMA knows. Current recovery thinking only has to pick up a book to find out. The government knows. It seems that the only people who don't know are the people suffering from the disease of alcoholism.

So how do you live with what seems to be the question of the increased-blood-sugar hour?

Simple. Let's do it . . .

Living Without Caffeine 101

Gotta start with tea because there is a universal confusion going on out there about tea and coffee and the amount of caffeine in them both.

Let's put it to rest once and for all.

Coffee has more caffeine than tea.

Tea has about fifty milligrams a cup, and coffee starts with 150 milligrams a cup . . .

So you want a coffee cutback plan. One way to begin would be to use tea. Have a cup of tea in between your coffees. But I've got some better suggestions for you in the *how to*'s of caffeine-withdrawals-without-feeling-horrible.

Again, start by cutting down slowly.

If you're a five-cups-a-day guy or gal—take it down to three! You could, if you wanted to run the marathon of withdrawal from caffeine, take it down to two.

It's very possible to cut way down on your caffeine if you use this little easy-to-maintain sobriety "cut back on caffeine over a period of time" method. You can expect to stop drinking the blood-sugar imbalancer without any major side effects.

First, it is imperative to understand what it is you are doing and why.

Make your plan.

And work the process. Take your time, do it over a month or two, and you can and will be caffeine free!

That's one way. The cut-back and cut-out way . . . Another?

Decaf it to death. Decaf has become an industry in itself lately, born from the need to cut back on caffeine. My thinking about decaf coffee has always been, what's the point? . . . If you don't get the buzz, why oh why drink it? But then again, this is coming from someone who couldn't for the life of me figure out why anyone would ever leave anything that resembles alcohol in a glass. But the fact is that the millions of people who drink decaf get the taste they oh so love, have the smell of coffee wafting through the house, and don't get the caffeine. So it's a thought.

Mix and match. The decaf way. Cut back on the "real" stuff . . . half-and-half?

From your five cups to your three, with one decaf in between? Be imaginative in your cutting back.

Caffeine in the morning, one cup, and then decaf it for the rest of the day?

That would be the most obvious and most common suggestion for cutting back on the dark brew . . . but I've got something on the wilder side for you. A thought, a

much more holistic, nineties thought, coffee substitutes—
ever heard of 'em?

Toasted grains, roots, and roasted nuts. They come in a
jar like coffee used to. You find them in health food stores
and in your grocery store. They've been around for years
and years for people who wouldn't drink coffee because
they understood long ago that shaky hands, heart palpita-
tions, raised cholesterol levels, sweaty palms, and nervous
conditions go along with a cup of . . . ? New market! The
people who are *choosing* not to drink coffee, not just people
who can't drink it, have created a whole new market.

The good coffee substitutes taste almost, not quite,
kind of like coffee.

No caffeine. No chemicals. No side effects. I don't like
'em, but you might. Give 'em a try and see what you think.

Another option in the free and "clear of caffeine" lifestyle that you might be getting more and more interested
in is herbal teas.

How about those folks that are always (they never
stop) suggesting herbal tea? I hate sleepy bear, mint mon-
key, seasoned berry, twinkle nightly teas . . . In my opinion, if you are going to do tea, do Earl Grey or nothing.
Put some lemon and honey in it and have a scone! Again,
up to you. Who knows, you may go from a seven-cup-a-
day coffee drinker to a twinkley nightly connoisseur! Good
on ya, mate. Whatever pleases your palate and doesn't
drop your blood sugar to your toes . . .

All of the above are reasonable suggestions for cutting
back your caffeine. Now I have some suggestions that "no
real coffee drinker in their right mind would ever consider," but I have to throw them out:

How about some . . . fresh veggie juice?

Yuk!

. . . fruit juices?

It's not coffee.

Oh come on, go for a cup of hot blackstrap molasses and water (get the hell out of here)—it's one of the coffee substitute suggestions of the nineties!

And there's always hot water and lemon (oh now that's something I'm looking forward to waking up to tomorrow morning . . .)

Why don't you just heat up your OJ (and I'm not referring to the murder—it's about time we get back to the drink when we say the initials, don't you think?)

You do want to cut back and eventually get rid of anything that's dropping your blood sugar to your toes. Because you want to get and stay sober. You want to feel better than you have in years. You want to support your body in healing, balance, looking and feeling great, and one way to do that would be to stop injecting an addictive drug that does blood-sugar damage. Simple. I've taken my own advice and I'm on the cut-down-and-out-coffee wagon myself!

So the truth is, there are three biggies when it comes to blood sugar, physical urges for alcohol, and you.

Refined sugar, refined white flour, and caffeine.

All tying into the blood-sugar connection. Scary! It's big for most of us because of all the emotional memories —ice cream, cake, coffee break—and now what?? Give it up? Live without it? OH, MY GOD . . . the love, the feelings, the comfort that go with it all . . . ? These are a few of our favorite things . . .

> **When the dog bites,**
> **When the bee stings,**
> **When I'm feeling bad,**
> **I simply remember my favorite things . . .**

AND THEN I DON'T EAT THEM ANYMORE???

That's not supposed to be the end of the song, but it is if you want to never drink again!

I'm going to ask the question before you do that's on so many minds right now—is life worth living without sugar, white flour, and caffeine? And then I'm going to answer it:

Yes, Yes, Yes, Yes, Yes.

Yep, more than you could imagine. Sober. Fabulous. Sober, balanced and restored is the best.

Going beyond the immediate satisfaction of ingesting the sugar, white flour, and caffeine and constructing the sober life you want is something that is nothing but a privilege to do.

Making decisions in your daily life that work for your end result. Hey, there's a thought.

Building the physical foundation you want. Why not? It's your life.

Staying sober and feeling well, not just being sober. What a great possibility.

Feeling whole, having energy, being balanced. Who could argue this? Who wouldn't want this?

It is right, it is possible, and it isn't difficult at all.

Just cut back on the habits that don't work for you and build the habits that do.

You have to take responsibility for your life, your health, and the state of your body and mind. If you choose to do it, you'll have a much better chance of accomplishing that life.

Managing your sobriety by understanding that what you put in your mouth absolutely, without a doubt, no chance in hell, can't deny it anymore, affects your body, your sobriety. The way you walk around feeling daily is an incredibly important part in the success of you not drinking.

It is the understanding and application of the solutions to the problems, that will make you more powerful than you could ever imagine. It's in this work that you will have the opportunity to live, feeling better than you have in years beyond *one day at a time!*

So let's say you are the blood-sugar-balancing queen or king. You've done the 360 in more biochemical areas of your life than you ever thought possible. Nobody could be as balanced as you, so . . . no problem, right? Never an urge. This staying stopped a breeze . . . Don't even think about drinking ever again?

Not so fast, sugarless boys and girls, because that ain't the way it works. Two things, side by side, equally important, both part of the sober plan—the physical and the mental. We have yet to talk about the mental. And we gotta . . . because, especially in the beginning of sobriety, you are gonna be calling on the mental sober plan as much as, if not more than, the biochemical stuff you need to pay attention to . . . It's a lot of work, this regaining your life, isn't it?

NO.

IT'S A LOT OF WORK LOSING YOUR LIFE. RE-GAINING IT IS A JOY!

‖‼‖

Voices

There are a few swift tricks of the sobriety trade. One is the mental work that does soooo much to support your life without alcohol, and you'll be calling on it often, so it's important to be familiar with, clear about, and very aware of. The first thing you need to be acutely aware of in your mentally sober world is voices. The voices of the monster. The addict's OH-SO-CONVINCING voice that is with you twenty-four hours a day.

Voices everywhere. Loud, convincing voices racing through your brain . . . Told ya it was mental work!

Here's what's gonna happen soon after you quit drinking forever. Within however long, you'll be at a friend's home, or driving past the old bar that you used to go to all the time, or sitting around during what used to be the perfect drinking time, and all of a sudden, out of nowhere, you are gonna hear voices. It's actually one, with a whole bunch of different personalities—big, loud, very, very convincing voices. It happens to every alcoholic I know, and it's gonna happen to you.

By the way, just for the record (and when did this deposition start?) everybody hears voices, not just us . . .

there's no question about that. It may not be talked about much in polite society (which isn't worth a shit anyway), but we all hear them.

"In our mind's ear we can literally hear ourselves talking to ourselves. You can hear one of your own voices right now as you read these words. It may sound something like yours, or it may sound the way you imagine this writer would sound. Quite often we create mental pictures to go along with the sound effects. We humans lead such rich inner lives!"

So right, that, Mr. Jack! the author of that great book —*The Small Book.*

We hear voices, all right, and when it comes to you not being able to be successful in giving up alcohol forever, you bet your ass you are gonna hear these voices.

Why the need to "get to know your monster's voice"? What's it got to do with you staying stopped drinking?

EVERYTHING.

GETTING TO KNOW YOUR ADDICTED VOICE, BEING SMARTER THAN IT IS, HAS EVERYTHING IN THE WORLD TO DO WITH WHETHER OR NOT YOU . . .

RELAPSE.

DRINK AGAIN.

JUST FIND YOURSELF, OUT OF NOWHERE, WITH A GLASS OF WINE IN YOUR HAND . . . DRINKING BEFORE YOU KNOW IT . . .

Because the truth of the *relapse* matter is, there is no such thing.

Let me give you a minute to digest that one because it seems on the surface to be a huge statement.

Remember, the hardest part about learning is . . . UNLEARNING.

I can certainly understand that you may be thinking right now that this comment is an unbelievable comment coming from the mouth of a woman who's already told you she has quit drinking a thousand times and gone back every time . . . otherwise known as relapse?

Yeah, I'm with ya. That is the way it seems on the surface. And here is another place where current recovery thinking and decades of research come together. Again I ask, why shouldn't it? Nothing but good can come from combining, including, broadening, eliminating what isn't true, and giving you more tools that work.

So let me say it again, there is no such thing as "drinking just happening" to you.

Let's talk about what *relapse* means.

Relapse is a slip or fall back into a former, worse state (as in illness).

Slip or fall. Like, off the wagon.

When I think of falling off a wagon, I think of falling, as in an accident. Don't you? *Fall* doesn't suggest intentional. There is nothing intentional about falling.

Listen to the expression. Who the hell would intentionally *fall off a wagon?* And what? Hit the road, given we are traveling on a wagon in a civilized country!

Fall off doesn't imply that whoever is doing the falling is in control, does it?

Slip? *Slip,* as in on ice? Not something anyone would deliberately do. Slip and fall, intentional? I don't think so.

Relapse intentional or something that just happens? An accident? Nope. Not when it comes to us drinking after we've stopped.

There's nothing accidental about it. We're not just walking along and all of a sudden, without ever knowing a thing, we fall into the bar.

Come on, it's not as if you are sitting at a table with friends and, like magic—you don't have a clue how—the beer got in your hands.

What, the beer just appeared?

You went into a coma and stayed there the whole time you were drinking? Nope. That's not how the staying stopped gets destroyed.

There is a ton of thought that goes into drinking again after you've quit, otherwise known as relapse. Truth is, it takes oodles of thinking, planning, and strategy to get the drink in your hand and start drinking again and this is where the voices come in.

This is where the voices come in. You, me, every alcoholic out there has the loudest, the most clear, as definite as definite can be voices going off in our head for hours before we drink. There's a three-hour play going on inside our heads before we ever say, "Yes, I think I'll have a glass of wine, please."

You've been "struggling" with it for hours before you "give in."

Beginning to see the advantage of learning more about your voices?

It's easy to figure how important it might be to get to know that voice, learn how to recognize it, become sooooooo very aware of it, what it's saying, how it's saying it, when it's saying it, so you can . . . ?

Do what?

Something . . . something to do with not drinking?

Something to do with building another voice?

Everything to do with you and your sobriety . . .

What do you think you need to do when something is seducing you into doing something you don't want to do . . . ?

Smack the hell out of it?

Walk away from it?

Tell it no?

Answer it back?

Represent what you want, not what your slimy seducer wants?

BACK TALK . . . what else would you do but talk back. . . .

Speak up.

Get connected to the decisions you've made, the life you want to build, the work you were doing before the rapist came to town.

Let your needs be known . . .

If you aren't going to answer back, who's going to? Who is going to represent what you the

mother/father
businesswoman/businessman
loving
wonderful

hardworking
fabulous
person . . .

want?

Speak up when your addictive voice is fighting for survival and doing everything in its power to convince you to drink . . . ? and you can bet it will, especially in the beginning of your sobriety, that's exactly what it's gonna do. It's gotta live and it can't if you don't drink.

That's worth repeating. Your addictive voice will die (eventually) if it isn't fed alcohol. You don't drink, it can't survive!

Your disease can't exist if you don't drink. This thing is fighting for survival in the beginning of your sobriety.

KNOW THAT!

So answer back, speak up, back talk . . . yell at the top of your lungs when you hear . . .

ADDICTIVE VOICE:

Just go ahead, have one. It really didn't get as bad as you think.

Here is an answer back:

YOU:

Didn't get as bad??? Let's walk through the last time I drank, shall we, Mr. Smooth Trying-to-Get-Me-to-Do-Something-That-Will-Destroy-My-Life Dude . . .

Walk through it. Tell the truth. Walk through the last time you drank. Be real clear and honest. Details. The truth. Could you imagine how advantageous it will be, talking back without shame or guilt? See your drinking for what it really was? Be clear about what really happened.

Think about the last time you drank, knowing that you have a disease and understanding something about that disease!

How great is that gonna be??? Walking through the truth of the "last" time without the self-flogging that normally happens AND with nutritional support!

Come on, it's easy to see how this new info can add soooo much support to sober living. Even the thought of being able to look back without the feeling of hopelessness, and the cravings, and knowing that you can stay stopped by using the information simply as a tool to maintain the sobriety that you treasure is going to be wonderful. And *doing* is better than you could ever imagine, even better than knowing.

You want the best sampling of an addictive voice you've ever heard, I'll give you mine. The most cunning. Soooooo persuasive. You don't get more convincing than my addictive voice . . . it's the same voice, of the same "infomercial queen," the voice that sells on TV, me. I sell for a living, so who do you think has the best sales swamp-monster voice in town? Me. My addictive voice could sell dog shit to a dog (a line, I might add, that I can't believe just came out of my mouth!). You wouldn't believe what I hear in my head.

It's been a rough week. Wouldn't a nice cold beer be wonderful right now?

You've worked soooo hard. Who deserves a beer more than you?

You've done really well in this sobriety thing. Why don't you have a beer and celebrate it? You've done it, now you know you can. (I swear I heard this the other day.) *You can get sober anytime you want to . . .*

And what I've learned to answer back . . .

A nice cold beer, as in one? Is that what you are suggesting I do? Why? It's never happened before. When I drink I don't have one, ever. I have ten, and if I choose to have one now, that's exactly what's going to happen. So, no thank you . . . and by the way, GO TO HELL!

The truthful answer to the simple first suggestion of *Hey, why don't you have a beer?*

There are quite a few different versions of the same untruth that blare in my head when it comes to having a beer, and as many different answers back.

Here's something that happens to me allllll the time . . . Pity poor, poor, pitiful me . . .

It's such a beautiful day at the beach. It's a pity you can't have a drink, like everyone else.

So what do I do? Well, let's define *pity*, shall we? And do more truth telling.

A pity? A pity I don't feed my addiction anymore? No. I don't see that as a pity. Actually, I'm happier now than I've ever been, I'm not feeding my disease that I was born with. I'm in control, not you. And by the way . . . GO TO HELL.

Ah, can't talk about voices without talking about my belligerent personality of the multiple swamp monster living in my head . . .

I'll give you a perfect example of the importance of identifying not only the voice, but which one it is.

Here's my belligerent addictive voice roaring . . .

Nobody can tell me what to do . . . I'm an adult. I can do what I want to . . . if I want to drink, I'm gonna.

And the real adult (not the alcoholic, diseased adult) answers right back . . .

True, true, how very true. I am an adult and I have made the decision that I want to make. This is my addiction talking, trying to convince me that I want to drink more than I want control of my life, and that's not true . . . This adult picks door number two, sobriety. OH, and by the way . . . GO TO HELL.

Can you see where this is leading? Relapse, accident, what do you think now?

Once I listened long enough to hear the damn drinking symphony that was going on in my head way, way, way before I picked up the drink, I began to understand the power I had and the power we all have.

By telling the truth about the drinking rehearsal that goes on in our brains, sometimes for hours, and the voice (with its many tones) screaming, suggesting, seducing, begging, luring you to drink, we have an unbelievable amount of power.

We have the power to

interrupt
change the direction
break old habits
create new ones
change the course of our lives

Too dramatic? I don't think so. That's what I've done. That's what thousands have done by listening, telling the truth, and answering back.

Powerless? Nope, not at all. Quite the opposite.

The power to stay sober is completely in your hands— whose hand is it that grabs the drink, anyway?

But you have to work it. Daily sober tricks of the trade.

While your body and mind are physically healing, while you are working your physical life, do the mental work. Pretty basic and as true can be!

Get to know your voice.

Know that any sign of, the slightest sound of it is about one thing—you drinking:

destruction
pain
hopelessness
fear
control
disease
death

Get to know it and . . .
ANSWER BACK.

Represent all the other you's. The minute you hear it, accuse it. Accuse the voice of the lying, destroying, manipulating that it has done or is doing in your life. Act the way you'd act if anyone or anything else in your life was doing those things to your life!!!

Let's go back to my brain for a second, shall we? Here's what happened to me the other day. I've been writing for a hundred years, at least that's what it felt like, that's all I'd been doing. Finishing the damn book. (That would be THIS damn book.)

Deadline. Pressure. Gotta get it done. The house. The kids. The dogs. The business. On and on and on and on and on . . .

And out of nowhere, a picture popped up in my brain.

"We think in pictures as well as sentences. So along with self talk, one may also 'see' the coming of the impulse. These are rehearsals of the alcoholic relapse.**"**

Innocent enough was what my Kodak moment was!

The little fun scenario started in my brain. The picture of the sunshine (I told ya, always with the sunshine and the beer!), tan, cool breeze, cold beer.

I am writing, and the pictures keep popping up in my brain.

I'm on a boat, water-skiing (which I do, and do quite well, till my back goes out). The sky is sapphire blue.

The sun—not Texas hot and muggy sun. We're talking San Diego, seventy-five and breezy sun, perfect sun!

Nobody is on the boat but my dearest friends. A few environmentalists on board, educating us all on how to become the most responsible, earth-friendly people. A macrobiotic chef has prepared the picnic basket, a sushi chef is arriving (by speedboat?) soon, and of course, there is nothing but the finest wine, the highest-quality beer, and Jewel IS about to sing, and Jewel IS one of my dearest friends (I don't think so. Never met her. But remember, this is my brain giving me a reason to drink, and it DOES go this far). She's suited up and about to break into song! The cream of the crop is on my boat. Full of stimulating conversation and laughter . . . HA, HA, HA, HA . . . it just doesn't stop. (Don't ever tell me that I can't paint a good drinking rehearsal!)

Fun, beer, joy, laughter, beer, fun, education, beer, fun, a perfect day!

Then the visual gets more dimensional. Because you can't call me a one-dimensional gal! The colors get brighter, the laughter gets louder. I hear it, I feel the breeze, smell the smells (coconut tanning lotion). It's all-inclusive . . . sexual (always with the sexual and the sunshine). He's there!

The man of my dreams, Al Pacino, is offering me a beer. Ready to take the top off my bottle with his teeth, if you know what I mean!

And it's all about one thing. Stop writing and drink.

Drink.

Drink.

Drink.

Drink.

Drink.

That's the message, and there are all kinds of presentations being given. The best sell in town. There is no better ad guy in the business. If it's a pitch that'll sell 'em all . . . call Alcohol Boy, 'cause there ain't any better in the business!

Visual and verbal all over the place in our brains before we ever pick up a drink, no question about it. And the good news? You can step in and refuse. You can easily expose the fantasy, tell the truth, and change the end result by walking through it . . . That's what one of the wonderful women in that very first, at my casa, meeting told me to do . . . Walk it through, Susan.

Walking It Through

Here's how you do it.

Don't be ashamed of anything. Just take the fantasy

that you are being presented, no matter what it is, and make it a reality by walking through the truth.

Then, you decide.

You decide if you want the reality of drinking.

And the only way to get to the reality of drinking is to tell more truth . . .

The truth about how bad it was AND how good it was. Gasp! I know, it sounds a little strange, but again, one moment, please, to see how much sense it really makes.

We must be very, very clear about the fantasy we are being offered in order to have a strong grasp on reality when the time comes.

It's get-to-know-your-fantasy-monster-voice time, folks.

Here's what your/my monster offers you: Good. Nothing but good. The best, the greatest situation every time.

The good parts of having a drink and only the good parts of drinking . . . and there are quite a few.

I learned something a long time ago—a new-in-sobriety trick of the sober trade—that helped me enormously. Check it out.

An ex-addict told me that we must give credit to the power of drinking if we ever want to stay stopped.

R̃ | *Give drinking credit?*

Yeah, just ask General Patton. (You don't think I'll go there, do ya, military-advice expert? Sure, why not? It's universal-principle stuff he based his tactics on. We can all go there—it's up for grabs.) You can't fight your enemy effectively until you know them or it!

Think about the advantage of understanding its ways. Seeing and knowing how it works. Learning everything there is to learn about how it manages, manipulates, maneuvers (the three M's of battle—new book?).

And most important of all, respect it.

Yeah, with everything you got inside of you, respect the hell out of the power this thing has. Respect what it was in your life, because until you do, you will be missing a huge part of the daily sober-living puzzle.

R Respect its power and acknowledge the good times.

It was fun. Drinking was fun, great fun. You had some of the best times of your life behind drinking. Right? True?

Maybe it did save you from social leprosy a hundred times. It was there for you when you just couldn't sum up the courage to be chatty and wonderful at that party full of fascinating people! It's supported you in some tough times, hasn't it?

Bending the elbow on many an afternoon absolutely took the cares of the day away.

And those romantic times, too numerous to count (who you been hanging with?), boy, weren't they great?

Remember when he put the ring in the champagne glass?

Oh, and that sunset, picnic, best-bottle-of-wine-you've-ever-tasted first kiss?

Running to the cabin for cover from the rain, wet, in love, and that hot toddy?

Get the drift?

What do you think your monster is gonna pull out of the memory basket—bad times? I don't think so. It'll be the great, great times of memory lane you'll be strolling down before you know it.

And one of the best tools-of-the-sober-trade way to stay that way is to tell both truths. All those times were fun, and they included alcohol.

How wonderful that kick is (and it is, in the beginning). How much fun you are going to have (and you are, for the first few hours). What a great feeling (true, true, true) it would be just to have a couple of drinks . . .

By understanding the power of alcohol, by giving it the respect it deserves, you can better support sobriety because only by telling the whole truth can you really tell the truth . . . OK, I'm not even gonna ask you to reread that or to suggest that it makes sense, but it's true!

The Power of Alcohol

The power of alcohol, let's talk about it . . .

I asked a guy who has five years sobriety and one of the worst twenty-plus years before of drinking that I've ever heard, and I've heard some drinking stories, but not like this!

Drinking beyond drinking is what he did. Nothing else mattered. Total saturation. Life was about drinking every day. He lost it all. Eight-day blackouts. The most talented human being, going right down the drain. Coulda been your son, throwing his life into the toilet completely and absolutely to do one thing, drink. That's all it meant, live to drink.

It only ended because he died.

He had an alcohol-induced seizure.

He had an out of body experience.

Rise up.

The angels, the whole thing . . .

So I thought he'd be a good person to ask about respecting the power of alcohol . . .

King Alcohol. That's what he calls it.

The biggest of the big.

"It's more powerful than any human being, any social status—or any element out there. Until you respect it for what it is, you will never have the tools you need to combat it.

"When someone kicks your ass in the playground or on the basketball court, one of the things that happens, after you brush yourself off, is you have a newfound respect for that person. You realize that you weren't as powerful in the situation as you thought you were. You will always remember the sting."

Here's one of the things we all need to do in order to stay sober, according to my friend:

"Give it the fucking respect it deserves. It kicked your ass."

See why I like this guy so much?

!!!

Appreciate it.

Appreciate the good it was in the beginning, the fun you had, and the truth of the ending. The truth about your disease. How it turned on you. How much fun it wasn't or isn't in the end. The friend that turned to Satan.

Both truths so that you can get to know your enemy.

Understand how it works.

Think how it thinks.

Watch how it lures you.

Learn its ways. Hear it, see it . . . and it's all very easy to do because this thing, your addiction to alcohol, does have a personality of its own. It has its own voice, very distinct, louder than you could ever imagine. It can be the most charming, the meanest, the most cunning. And it will do whatever it needs to do to get you to drink . . .

So, what do you do?

Come on, think about it, General Patton Juniors. You are gonna ANSWER BACK. Represent the you that doesn't want to drink, the you that isn't interested in getting high right now, the rational you that is you, the responsible and unaddicted you that is you and will never be addicted to this stuff again because you ain't gonna drink it.

And start your own little production!

I got ya rehearsal in my brain!

You answer back, that's what you do.

You may be in the hallway warming up, in the beginning, while the monster has the main hall. So what?

Eventually you'll be playing the main room. It's been around longer. The monster's voice is much, much louder than the other "you" voices right now. It's smoother. Better trained. You are up against one hell of a well-developed voice. A practiced voice. Operatic in its size. One with its own audience (your life) that has been coming to its performances for years. Your other voice is weak. So?

Strengthen it.

Strengthen it by using it.

Do your own voice lessons. Use them daily, every minute, hourly.

Practice, practice, practice . . .

Your other voice isn't as sure, as secure, as comfortable as Opera Boy is.

Answer back no matter how it sounds.

No matter how you feel, speak up.

The only way to build confidence is to have the guts to get up and do it (whatever it is, by the way). It is in the practice of doing . . .

Make your whisper a roar.

Project the you that wants more from your life than to live for your disease.

Work it.

Develop it.

And before you know it . . . you'll be playing the Met and *it*'ll be in the Catskills in the old-timers' room . . .

I've got a little story of a bus ride for ya. A bus ride in my brain. The bus ride of my life, if you will (or want to—help me), one of the most helpful tools of the sober trade that my therapist, Mark, taught me and one that I still use alllll the time.

Think *speed one* (of course I didn't have such a commercial reference when I was doing this little mental imagery, but you do) in your own head. The bus. Out of control. Danger, danger, danger, and guess who's driving your out-of-control bus?

Your addiction.

And the other passengers?

You, the———? Fill in the blank:

mother
businesswoman
husband
father
friend

Fill in your own description . . .
Anything you want to be.
Everyone you are.
All the you's that live in your life . . .
Because every damn one of them is on the bus that
the addict is driving!

If you don't want to die, someone has to take the wheel
from the addict and get control of the bus.

Who's it gonna be? Any other one of the you's is fine.
If there was anything that does need to be at the back of
the bus, quite literally, with everything that horrific statement implies, it's your addict. Put it there. Take control of
the wheel and steer the thing in the direction you want it
to go.

!!!!

The beast never goes away. That is not something to
be frightened of, it is just something to be very, very
aware of. It gets weaker and weaker. You get better and
better at spotting it, answering back, and always representing you.

Within a very short period of time you'll find yourself
actually laughing out loud when you hear some of its suggestions.

You may even find yourself, like I did, saying things in
public around complete strangers, like:

*What are you, out of your damn mind? That's not the
way it goes, big boy.*

*Oh, my God, how far are you gonna go with the grass
skirt and the ski boat?*

*Could you at least hand me something higher quality
than Maui? South of France, maybe I'd pick up a
drink. But Maui in August? Forget about it, asshole . . .*

If you find this happening in front of strangers, do
what I did and tell them you have a sentence form of
Tourette's syndrome. But you get what I'm saying. It gets
funny. You will be in control before you know it. Drinking
will never just happen to you without you knowing way,
way before that there is a Broadway-size rehearsal going
off in your brain!

When you have the nutritional support we all so desperately need, and as you get to know your monster, the
enemy, and begin to answer back, you will find . . . two
years later, ten years later, you will be able to pass your
"favorite" drinking situation and it will flash in your brain,
Hey, how about a drink?, you will find that your recovery
time gets faster and faster and faster in your ability to
answer back.

What was an all-consuming thing becomes a split second of a thought because your brain will be so full of your
life.

What had so much fear behind it forever will have
laughter, awareness, power, and a wonderful sense of
peace. The peace anyone feels when they know they are
protected and safe. You watching out for you. You pro-

tecting your life. Someone representing the other people on the bus.

So, plan nutritional support, be aware of sugar, white flour, caffeine, voices, and what's next? Wellness and sobriety.

Wellness and Sobriety

Wellness is one of the most abused words in our world. Like *love, wellness* can mean a million different things to a million different people. So, to make your life in sobriety easier, we are going to take my definition of *wellness* and live by it, OK?

How well you are very much depends on how you live. How you live, as in how you eat, how you breathe, and how and if you move.

I've been talking this stuff for a long, long time, and bringing it up in a discussion about sobriety isn't me tooting my own horn. It isn't a filler, and it's got nothing to do with weight loss. This is some of the most important information you are going to get when it comes to the power of you managing your own life.

We've already made the all-important connection between what you put into your mouth, your blood sugar, and your craving for alcohol. Interesting stuff, for sure, but it ain't nothing (well, it is very, very important—I mean *nothing* in the must-make-a-point way) compared to what else food can do for you and your new sober existence.

Wellness is about living. It has a whole lot to do with how you live, the quality of your life, how long you live . . .

Don't even think of telling me we don't have control over disease.

Eighty-five percent of all disease can be directly attributed to lifestyle. Hello, AMA fact. Eighty-five percent??? That means we have a whole lot of control over whether or not we drop like flies from

> heart disease
> stroke
> cancer
> diabetes
> obesity

or just spend our daily lives in a slow, steady decline down. Living with no energy? Not enough strength to get through your day? Chronically exhausted?

Alcoholics Anonymous has a saying:

> **HALT. Never get too**
> **hungry**
> **angry**
> **lonely**
> **and tired.**

Great advice, and we can add to it.

The *hungry* and *tired* part of that statement has soooo very much to do with the foods you are eating. The quality of the food you are living on. The fuel you are putting into your body.

How often you are fueling? Otherwise known as the *eat* part of the wellness formula.

• • •

Let's talk about eating.

In our world, the United States of America, 1997, we don't eat food. We live on chemical, fast, processed-beyond-recognition junk. Total crap, and remember the old saying, "Crap in, crap out!"

Tired and eating connected? I think so, and I know you do too . . .

Tired first, because our blood sugar drops to our toes. Been there, done that. It's time to move on.

You might also be tired because this junk that we live on is . . .

Dead food. Not live. Dead. Nutritionally void. We've heard it before, but now let's make the *nutritionally void* and *tired* connection, and in order to do that it's time to ask some real basic questions.

Nutrition, what is it?

What does it mean for your body?

How important is it?

Nutrients are what your body lives on.

Your body doesn't produce nutrients.

It is your job to make sure that your body has what it needs to live.

If you don't do that, your body withers . . . It'll live, but about as well as half the people I see at the mall are living. Not very well.

We have a twofold goal here, you and I, us alcoholics.

Number One, we have to rebuild. We have to rebuild the zillions of cells that are tired, hungry. The organs that have been abused and abused and abused are definitely tired and very, very hungry for nutrients. Organs live on food. Organs function on the nutrition that is in the foods we eat.

That brain of yours doesn't need good fuel? We know good and well what the bad food, alcohol fuel, has done to your brain. It only stands to reason that some good, highest-quality-gasoline-in-the-land, nutrient-filled-food fuel would be very, very important to your sobriety.

That's the first thing we have to do. The second is maintain. Live differently. Support sobriety. Move forward. Change the things that support drinking and develop the lifestyle habits that support sobriety.

Giving our bodies

energy
fuel
wellness
nutrients
life

And the best place to begin is by getting the answer to the question . . .

What is good food?

Again, if you want to be abused, look at the *good for you.*

Healthy? What isn't!

Low-fat, lean, light: everything is!

Read any food labels lately? *Healthy* is the word. Everything seems to be *healthy!* At least that's what they are alllllll using, those food-manufacturing boys, to get you to pick up their product. So, there is a bit of confusion out there, but don't let it stop ya, because it's easy to clear up.

Good food is whole food.

Processed is OK once in a while. (Keep in mind the different kinds of processed you are already an expert on:

bleached white flour muffin or organic cornmeal muffin—which is the higher-quality processed food?) But to live on processed foods is one of the worst things you can do for your health.

Processed means *broken down. Processed* means *altered.* Less than the original. Damaged? Yep. Look at the difference between french fries and a baked potato. The difference is sliced, salted, dipped in carcinogenic boiling oil, fried to a heart-clogging crisp—or whole food with skin, with nutrients, with fiber, with water, with minerals, slow to digest, wonderful fuel that lasts. Fuel that gives you energy. Fuel that helps you do your work. Fuel that helps keep your blood sugar balanced. You tell me.

It's not a difficult connection to make. As soon as you have a look at nutrition, good food, whole food, and see it for what it really is—it is beyond simple to eat well.

Does it grow that way? Ask the question. And eat more foods that do.

Sorry, it's no more complicated than that.
Eat more whole food.

whole
live
fresh
food

You know what that means? A bowl of brown rice once in a while—hey, who couldn't use a good colon cleaning every couple of days?

Grains

Let's talk grains. Whole grains. When is the last time you ate some?

That whole-wheat bread that you had for breakfast yesterday isn't a whole grain. It is a processed food. Ever seen a bread-tree? Once in a while with that processed stuff, and much, much more of the whole-grain stuff—that's where we are heading in our sober life.

Whenever I ask the "last time you ate a grain" question, especially to alcoholics, I get a blank stare.

The last time a grain went into your body, doing all the wonderful things grains do—feed, clean, absorb, and eliminate—when was it?

OK, I think I know the answer, so let's just get to the solution: *How to Include More Life-Supporting Grains in Your Life,* by Susan Powter.

Rice for breakfast. Why not?

Take a walk on the wild-rice side every once in a while. Fabulous!

Stir-fry anytime.

Rice pilaf. Not the Roni stuff we grew up with. Real rice pilaf. Make a ton, stick it in the fridge. It'll be there for ya all week.

You can salt it and pepper it.

You can soy sauce it.

You can curry it.

You can oregano and thyme it.

You can dessert it . . .

Dessert it ! ! ! rice raisin pudding.

Rice with fresh baked apples. Had that for breakfast a couple of mornings ago . . .

You can stuff with it.

What, are you kidding . . .?

Tomato with rice stuffing, YUUUUUMMMMMM.

Eggplant to the nines.

Bell peppers stuffed with life-giving rather than heart-disease-giving . . . get it? Making some sense here, isn't it?

There's nothing complicated about including more grains in our severely grain-depleted Western diet. It's just a food that we are not as familiar with as Gummi Bears, that's all . . .

Ever even tried barley? Nothing like a good barley soup recipe.

Oats. Think about trying the original food, oat groats. They're much better than the processed version, oatmeal.

Quinoa. Not the famous actress who has the short black hair and the most perfect skin on the planet—that would be Winona. Quinoa is a grain.

Easy to make and oh so versatile.

In salads. It doesn't get much better than to boil it up and throw it all over.

You'd be surprised how quickly you become familiar with foods that you never, ever thought you'd be able to pronounce, let alone eat! Like bulgur. Sounds gross, but there's nothing gross about this little cracked wheat of a grain. It cooks like rice, but it's a little nutty—not in its behavior, in its flavor.

You think rice pilaf is good?? Go nuts and make some bulgur pilaf the next time you are hankering for pilaf.

One bulgur recipe that has mainstreamed a bit in the last few years is tabbouleh.

Cooked bulgur with fresh lemon juice, onions, parsley, salt, and pepper, and you've got one of the best salads you've ever tasted.

So refreshing.

So filling.

So whole food and sobriety supporting . . .

So much better than the refined-white-sugary, processed, non-food crap most of us have been putting into our bodies!

Eat more grains and stay stopped drinking.

Oh, yeah . . .

When the skeptics come knocking, tell 'em:

"From a nutritional standpoint grains are the most valuable of all foods." And then explain to them that you need food to live and you are choosing higher-quality food than you did when you were drinking.

When they continue to try and convince you that you are out of your mind by even suggesting that high-quality fuel/food has anything to do with you and your sober life, then tell 'em:

"Grains are full of protein, carbohydrates, fiber, vitamins and minerals."

Go ahead and throw in the fact that "whole grains are nothing but layers and layers of nutrition."

And maybe, if you are kind enough, you may take a moment to explain all this over a bowl of . . . or maybe not! The most important thing here is that you understand. That your body gets everything it needs to heal and grow.

You need to know, for your life, that including grains in your daily food intake can do nothing but support the best of health. If you want to protect the commitment you've made in sobriety, help your body heal, rebuild, be strong, cleaner, function better than it has in years, eat more grains. It's sound, proven, easy-to-understand advice that will make an enormous difference in the way you look and feel.

Veggies

Now let's talk veggies. Can't talk whole food without talking veggies. No can do.

Vegetables are whole foods. Vegetables are one of our most important foods. Health and vitality are dependent on them.

And guess where most of us get our veggies from. The can. The frozen food section. The veggie section in the instant dinner.

That's not exactly what we are talking about when we say "to enliven," which is the definition of the Latin word for *vegetables*. You wouldn't exactly say anything on a TV dinner tray could enliven.

They would be veggies, but you couldn't say they were fresh or the highest quality.

Steamed zucchini with salt and pepper. Juicy, tasty, and fabulous.

Brussels sprouts can't taste good? Not true when you blanket them in lemon mustard sauce.

Sweet potato. Loaded, loaded, loaded with vitamins, and have you ever tasted anything as good as the sweetest of potatoes with a squirt of orange juice and cinnamon! No, you haven't, 'cause it's some kind of good. Nothing boring about it.

Cabbage isn't just cabbage when you use it as the main ingredient, with fresh ginger, a touch of rice vinegar, and sliced carrots. No, no, no, it's not just cabbage anymore!

Tomatoes . . .

Scallop 'em.

Bake 'em.

Stuff 'em.

Fresh with a little salt.

Pie it . . .

Squash corn pie.

Succotash pie.

Veggie melody pie.

Spinach pie.

Potato pie . . . fluffy, warm, comforting, creamy.

What??? This is bad food? Not at all.

Veggies. You want veggies?

Veggie lo mein. I'm there.

Whole wheat pizza with a ton of grilled veggies. Count me in.

Corn on the cob. You can always find that.

Baked potato. They are everywhere.

Salad bar. You can always find one and load up . . .

There is nothing like a veggie soup. Take it with you wherever you go . . . Hey, come on, if it helps you stay stopped and all you gotta do is make sure you've got some great fuel/food with you, what's so difficult about that? Nothing.

When it comes to vegetables, think flavors, think colors, think texture, think about how much life is in this food and be a veggie whiz . . .

There is more to life than just steaming 'em . . .

Sautéing in water. You don't even have to ever use oil.

Grill.

Marinate and grill. You wouldn't believe the imagina-

tive things you can do (or have done in your favorite restaurant) when it comes to grilling whole veggies.

Roast 'em.

Sandwich them.

Soup them.

Casserole them.

Dip 'em . . . Just do them. Do more veggies. They are
nature's provision for and answer to every single vitamin,
mineral, and fiber need our body has. Simple. That is the
truth. It's an easy truth to live by and nobody can argue
with it.

And there is just one more thing on our path to better
fueling . . .

Whole, real, grown that way, and . . .? Gassy. (Only
till your body learns how to digest real, versus processed,
stripped food.) Beans.

Beans

What a food!

Loaded with more protein than any other food in the
veggie kingdom, without the cholesterol and saturated fat
of some OTHER forms of protein that we are, unfortunately, much more familiar with.

Remember our discussion about carbs, simple sugar,
your blood sugar, and all that? Well, complex carbs means
slower breakdown, fabulous fuel, long-lasting fuel . . . and
if it's a complex carbohydrate you are in the market for to
keep your body balanced and well, you don't get better
than beans.

I think the word *whole* was designed with the bean in mind, quite honestly, because when it comes to the bean, there is not an ounce of processing going on.

The soybean grows in its pod. You depod and eat it.

    navy beans
    black-eyed peas
    garbanzos
    lima
    great northern beans
    kidney beans
    lentils
    split peas
    black turtle
    adzuki beans
    pinto

No processing involved and packed with fiber beyond fiber, potassium, calcium, iron, vitamin A, magnesium, phosphorus, vitamin C, and on and on it goes because beans are a wonderful food, there's no question about that.

And this wonderful food is a food that we (Americans) have no clue what to do with.

The whole-grain question—"When's the last time you had one?"—at least gets an answer. The bean question— "When's the last time you had a bean?"—gets a foul face and "yuck" for a response and always gets a gas joke.

It's a food that may be a little harder to get into the consciousness of our instant all-American diets, but it's not going to be difficult anymore. I consider this a quest. Jonny Quest (do you remember that cartoon? and his dog

—what was its name?). *The Path to Enlightenment and the Bean,* by Susan Powter.

The Bean and You, by me.

The Bean and Your Colon . . . OK, I've gone too far. How out of character.

It's time to understand the bean, and here's what you have to do to include this wonderfully rich, healthy, balanced food in your daily life.

Let's just make something that is unfamiliar as familiar as it can be . . . more American? I thought I'd Yankee Doodle this to death by bringing up the historical connection between beans and the UNITED STATES OF AMERICA, the citizens of. Purple mountain majesty, along the fruited (whole-food reference right in one of our national anthems? hello, how much more proof do you need!) plains. Let's go . . .

Boston baked beans	Tea Party mean anything to you?
navy bean soup	There's the army, the air force, the marines, and the . . . ?
senate bean soup	Without which there would be no laws passed!
cowboy chili	Where do you think that came from, India?
three-bean salad	What would a deli be without it? Not a deli, that's for sure!
bean loaf	Oh sure, where do you think the meat got the idea from?

See, see, see the connection? Beans are as all-American as you get! So let's get them into our bodies, our lives, our sober living!

It's not difficult to get the benefit of beans into your body because this is one of the most versatile foods you can get.

You can . . .

soup them
stew them
mash them
bake them
sprout them
top them
loaf them
include them in any meal or make them a meal of
   their own

Easy, easy, easy to find, easy to cook 'em, easy to store 'em, easy to pay for 'em (nothing expensive about beans), and it's really, really easy to understand why you need them.

Check Diagram Man. Go back and look at the truth about the nutritional damage that alcohol does. Look at the information about whole real foods—the vitamins, the minerals, the fiber, the energy they offer, and how badly our bodies need all of it—then look at the bean.

Compare the nutrients in beans, vegetables, and grains to the labels on the instant, processed, enriched non-foods that you may be eating way too much of, and you decide for yourself. Which supports your sobriety? Which will help you get what you want—healing, life, energy, strength?

Exercise

Combining one career move with another—fitness expert and drunk? No. That's not what's going on when I'm talking about fitness, exercise, building lean muscle mass, oxygen, cardio-endurance, and sobriety. What's happening is you are about to get some of the best sober-advice, protection, common-bloody-sense daily guidelines. Something you can easily do, the application of how to do it, and prevention for staying the way you want to stay. Sober.

Here's what exercise does:

sweats out toxin
oxygenates all of the organs in your body
creates a more efficient machine
strengthens
supports
enforces life (without oxygen, how far can you go?)
builds
develops
prevents
protects
stimulates
invigorates
relaxes

Thanks very much. Chapter closed? What else is there to say? Why wouldn't you include fitness in your daily sober plan? It makes soooo much sense.

BUILDING LEAN MUSCLE MASS

Let's talk about building lean muscle mass. The most met-abolically active tissue in the body.

Metabolically, the most active. Big, big statement when it comes to your body functioning well, really, really well.

And the importance of an active, healthy metabolism is? Well, the best way to understand the importance of it is to be real clear about the effects of not having a healthy metabolic rate and what that means in your life.

Your metabolic rate has everything to do with the en-ergy you have or don't have. If your metabolic rate is func-tioning like a slug, you will be a slug. And millions are.

Think *healthy metabolism,* think *endurance.*

Think *metabolic rate that is slow,* think *sludge.*

Now think, if you will, about eating tons of processed junk with no nutritional support and, to top it off, sludge for energy . . .

How do you think your life in sobriety will be—easier, or harder? More of a fight? Less supported? Less possi-ble???

A connection that is easily made, and now that we have, aren't you dying to know how to get it?

You gotta build it. Building lean muscle mass is done by using resistance. Dumbbells. You don't ever have to worry about getting bulky (the most common reason why women are afraid to pick up the old dumbbell), because it takes hundreds of pounds of weights, years and years, the most unbelievably unhealthy diet, a little too much tanning, and a few steroids here and there to achieve that very unattractive look that you see on the front of muscle and scantily-clad-bikini-gal mags!

Have no fear, my friends, if it's bulk you are worried about, get fat. Fat is bulky. Fat people are wide, not lean strong people.

The advantages of you building some upper-body, abdominal, and lower-body lean muscle mass in your sober life are:

> You will be able to eliminate some (a lot) of the poisons you've built up.
> You will feel stronger because you are stronger.
> You certainly will look and feel better than you have in a hundred years.

Building lean muscle mass is one of the most important elements in achieving fitness.

AEROBICS

Why would ya? Neon leotards? Well actually, truth be known, that was more Dallas in the eighties. If you want the newest in exercise looks, come to L.A. in the nineties and you'll find Dad's dirty boxers, weight vests, lots and lots of spinning (and I mean that quite literally, folks), still with the music fast and loud and the attitude not improved at all—but point being, why would ya . . .?

> Jump around like an idiot.
> Step and hop.
> Circuit class.
> Cross-training.
> Indoor and outdoor bedlam.

I, better than anyone you'll ever meet, understand the hesitation. Again, it's easy to clear up. Let's just get down to the facts and how to apply this life-giving stuff to yours . . . life, that is!

The definition of *aerobic* is any movement at all for thirty minutes or more in oxygen.

Why be in oxygen? Because oxygen equals life. Don't believe me? Hold your breath for five minutes and see how well you do.

Aerobic gets oxygen to every cell and muscle in your body. Why get oxygen to every cell and muscle in your body?

Cellular damage?

Organs been hurting?

Irritated?

Sick?

Unwell?

How about that opium den of yours? Oxygen have anything to do with how you feel, how you think, whether or not you can? Again, hold your breath and see! Of course it does. And you/me/we all need as much oxygen as we can get.

So if you want to get aerobic and get the benefits of, the question would be, how do you know if you are in oxygen?

Movement for thirty minutes in oxygen means you are not out of breath while you are moving. In oxygen is being able to talk, finish a sentence, while you are doing your aerobic activity; out of oxygen means sucking wind, blue in the face, huffing and puffing, or what most people have been doing during the class!

And movement:

walking
hiking
aerobics/dance/yoga
exercise classes
biking
running
swimming

These are all aerobic if you are doing them for thirty minutes or more and if you are in oxygen while you are doing them.

Aerobic is very, very important in maintaining good health, increasing cardio-endurance, heart-lung capacity, circulation, oxygenating the blood, healthy cell life. It has everything to do with your energy level, how your body processes, cleaning, and coating your brain with a much better buzz than you ever got from alcohol. (OK, maybe not quite as good as that great kick, but you catch my drift?) Your brain will be flooded with morphinelike chemicals called beta-endorphins that get you high, and isn't that what we all like to do?

on top of the world
ready for the day
energized
grounded
well

That's why you need to exercise.

But let's get real. Who has the time? Who really wants to? And what kind of reality are we talking about? From drinking to fitness (I went about it the other way around), is it really possible?

Yes it is. If you understand that you don't need to train for a triathlon. All you need to do is start by moving in oxygen for thirty minutes or more consistently.

That means go for a walk today.

If you want to go fitness mad and throw in thirty minutes of upper-body weight training with some dumbbells, there it is, a great hour (one bloody hour, that's all) of fitness that will benefit you enormously and support you tremendously.

And if it's motivation and inspiration you're looking for, I can easily nutshell the best motivational, inspirational advice you've ever heard (a little cocky, would you say?) when it comes to your new life in wellness.

If you're looking for motivation or waiting to find it before you start exercising, you will never start. Don't wait till you are motivated to go for the walk. Go for the walk. Motivation is in the doing. In the practice. It is one of the results of getting well. You are never going to bump into it. It isn't "out there somewhere." Your unfit body isn't going to wake up tomorrow and say, "Yippeee, let's go for a run!" It can't be excited about that. It's unwell, it doesn't have the cardio-endurance necessary to do it. You have to build it. Slowly. Within oxygen. One fitness level to the next and the next and the next . . . that would be one fitness level at a time . . . New step, old saying!

It couldn't be more basic than that, could it? Change the things that support craving alcohol and start supporting sobriety! Bingo. You'd think that would have been mentioned a long, long time ago (like the beginning of a

Don McLean song?) but it wasn't, so it's time now to stand up and say:

WHAT WE EAT AND HOW MUCH WE EXERCISE ABSOLUTELY AFFECTS THE WAY WE FEEL. AND THE WAY WE FEEL CAN HAVE SO VERY MUCH TO DO WITH OUR SOBRIETY.

That's the bottom (and a lean one at that) line!

Here's to your sober life being a little easier—some recipes from me to you.

Recipes

Check out my recipes with all of the wonderful ingredients that we have been talking about: whole grain, veggies, and beans. And they cut back on sugar.

GRAINS

!!!! *Millet and Vegetable Casserole*

> *1 Tbsp olive oil*
> *1 medium onion, finely chopped*
> *4 cloves garlic, minced*
> *1 stalk celery, sliced*
> *1 medium green pepper, cut into strips*
> *2 carrots, thinly sliced*
> *2 small zucchini, cut in half and sliced into*
>   *½-inch slices*
> *2 tomatoes, peeled and chopped*
> *1 c millet*

> *2 c boiling vegetable broth*
> *2 tsp fresh ginger, minced*
> *1½ tsp curry powder*
> *1½ tsp salt, or to taste*
> *½ tsp black pepper*

1. Heat oil in a large frying pan. Add onion, garlic, celery, green pepper, carrots, zucchini, tomatoes, and ginger. Sauté the vegetables for 5 minutes, stirring often.
2. Meanwhile, wash the millet thoroughly, changing water often, and let drain for 10 minutes.
3. In a dry skillet over medium heat, toast the millet lightly, stirring constantly.
4. To the vegetables, add millet, broth, curry, salt, and pepper. Mix all ingredients well. Cover pan and simmer for 10 to 15 minutes, until the liquid is absorbed.
5. Adjust seasoning and serve.

Try this one—you'll be surprised.

SERVING SIZE: 14 OZ
Servings per recipe: 4
Calories: 281
Total fat: 6 g
Saturated fat: 1 g

Fat 19%
Protein 11%
Carbohydrate 70%

!!!! *Very Corny Corn Muffins*

> 1 c whole-wheat pastry flour
> 1 c yellow cornmeal
> 4 tsp baking powder
> ½ tsp salt
> ¼ c sugar
> 1 large whole egg
> 2 egg whites
> 1¼ c 1% milk
> 2 tbsp canola oil
> 1 c canned cream corn

1. Preheat oven to 425°.
2. In a bowl, combine dry ingredients.
3. In another bowl, combine egg, egg whites, milk, oil, and corn.
4. Stir wet ingredients into dry ingredients until they are just moist. Do not overmix.
5. Lightly grease a muffin tin or use 12 paper muffin cups or use a nonstick muffin tin. Spoon mixture into cups.
6. Bake in oven for 20 to 25 minutes, until muffins are golden brown.

Fabulous with soups and stews—really moist and sweet.

SERVING SIZE: 3 OZ
Servings per recipe: 12
Calories: 152
Total fat: 3 g
Saturated fat: 1 g

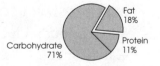

▐▀▀ *Brown Rice Pilaf*

    1 Tbsp olive oil
    2 medium onions, chopped
    6 cloves garlic, minced
    10 oz mushrooms, sliced (canned or fresh)
    ½ tsp thyme
    1½ c brown rice, uncooked
    5¾ c boiling chicken broth
    1 tsp salt, or to taste
    ½ tsp black pepper, or to taste

1. Preheat oven to 350°.
2. Heat oil in a 3-quart ovenproof casserole on medium heat. Sauté onions and garlic for 10 minutes, until onions are transparent.
3. Add mushrooms and thyme. Raise heat and sauté mushrooms until liquid evaporates.
4. Add rice and mix until rice turns opaque.
5. Add broth, salt, and pepper. Cover casserole tightly and cook in oven for 1 hour. Check to see if all the liquid is absorbed.
6. Fluff with a fork and serve.

Fabulous as a stuffing!

Serving size: 13 oz
Servings per recipe: 6
Calories: 230
Total fat: 4 g
Saturated fat: 1 g

Fat 16%
Protein 10%
Carbohydrate 74%

VEGETABLES

▌▐▐▌ *Roasted Vegetables*

> 3 carrots, quartered lengthwise and then cut in half
> 4 medium zucchini, quartered lengthwise and then cut in half
> 2 small sweet potatoes, peeled and cut into ¼-inch circles
> 2 large onions, cut into 6- or 8-inch wedges
> 1 green pepper, cut into 1-inch strips
> 1 red pepper, cut into 1-inch strips
> ¼ c chopped garlic
> 2 Tbsp olive oil
> 2 tsp crushed rosemary
> 1 Tbsp kosher salt
> 1 tsp pepper, or to taste
> Pam for spraying pan
> 4 c cooked brown rice

1. Preheat oven to 400°.
2. Cut vegetables and place in a large bowl. Add garlic, oil, spices, salt, and pepper. Use your hands to mix thoroughly.
3. Spray 2 sheet pans with Pam; wipe excess off with paper towel. Place vegetables in a single layer. Place one pan on bottom shelf of oven and the other on the top shelf. Rotate every 20 minutes to be sure they brown evenly on top and bottom. Cook for 45 minutes to 1 hour, checking every 20 minutes.

4. Serve with your favorite grain. This is good to eat as a snack at room temperature.

Options

Change seasonings to your favorites. You can also use string beans and mushrooms, left whole.

Eat plain or with pasta, in salads, on sandwiches, in fajitas, or add to any Italian dish. Or grill instead for a barbecue.

Incredible! Great rosemary flavor.

SERVING SIZE: 23 OZ
Servings per recipe: 4
Calories: 382
Total Fat: 3 g
Saturated fat: 1 g

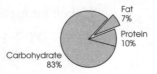

Fat 7%
Protein 10%
Carbohydrate 83%

!!!! *Potato and Vegetable Soup*

4 cloves garlic, minced
1 large onion, chopped
1 Tbsp canola oil
3 medium russet potatoes, peeled and cubed
2 medium carrots, cut in half lengthwise and sliced
2 medium celery stalks, sliced
7 c chicken broth
2 c frozen peas
   handful of egg noodles
1 Tbsp fresh dill, or 1 tsp dried
¼ c chopped fresh parsley
3 tsp salt, or to taste
½ tsp pepper, or to taste

1. In a large soup pot over medium-high heat, sauté onion and garlic in the oil for 7 minutes, or until soft.
2. Add potatoes, carrots, and celery, and mix well. Continue stirring for 2 minutes.
3. Add broth and bring to a boil. Lower heat and simmer for 30 minutes, or until the potatoes are ready to fall apart.
4. Add peas, noodles, dill, parsley, salt, and pepper. Cook 5 more minutes, until noodles are done. Correct seasoning and enjoy.

Option

Leave out the dill and parsley, and it's still the best.

Tastes like "Mom's-great-old-fashioned-stew-on-the-farm."

SERVING SIZE: 17 OZ
Servings per recipe: 6
Calories: 187
Total fat: 3 g
Saturated fat: 0 g

Fat 14%
Protein 15%
Carbohydrate 71%

¡¡¡¡ *Minestrone Soup*

> 1 Tbsp olive oil
> 1 c thinly sliced onion
> 6 cloves garlic, minced
> 1 c diced carrots
> 1 c diced celery
> 2 medium zucchini, diced
> 3 c shredded cabbage
> 2 tsp oregano

1½ tbsp basil
2 tsp salt, or to taste
½ tsp black pepper, or to taste
6 c chicken or vegetable broth
1 28-oz can tomatoes with juice
1½ c canned cannelini or Great Northern beans, rinsed
    and drained
2 c water
1 c whole grain or vegetable elbow or ditalini pasta

1. Heat oil in large pot over medium heat. Add onion and garlic, and sauté until soft. Add carrots and celery, and cook for 5 minutes.
2. Add zucchini, stir well, and cook for 2 to 3 minutes.
3. Add cabbage and cook 5 more minutes.
4. Add oregano, basil, salt, and pepper. Cook 2 more minutes. Add broth and tomatoes, lower heat, and cook for 2 to 2½ hours, uncovered.
5. Add canned beans and water. Continue cooking for 15 to 20 minutes.
6. Cook elbows or ditalini in boiling salted water for 8 to 10 minutes, or until done. Add drained pasta to soup and stir well. Serve.

Wonderful on a cold winter night! Leave out the pasta and you can freeze it.

SERVING SIZE: 18 OZ
Servings per recipe: 10
Calories: 175
Total fat: 2 g
Saturated fat: 0 g

Fat 10%
Protein 18%
Carbohydrate 72%

⁙ *Chinese Stir-fry Vegetables*

> 2 tbsp cornstarch
> Soy-Ginger Sauce (see recipe)
> 2 tbsp dark sesame oil
> 2 medium onions, cut into
>   ¼-inch slices
> 3 carrots, cut on the diagonal into slices; and then
>   slices cut into matchsticks
> 1 head broccoli, stem peeled, sliced, and cut, and
>   florets cut small
> 12 black Chinese mushrooms, soaked for 20 minutes in
>   hot water, stems removed, and cut into ¼-inch strips
> 2 medium red peppers, cut into ¼-inch strips
> 4 c cooked brown rice

1. Add cornstarch to Soy-Ginger Sauce and stir until smooth. Set aside.
2. Heat oil in a heavy pan. Sauté onions for 5 minutes. Add carrots and broccoli, and cook for 10 minutes. Add mushrooms and peppers, and cook for 3 minutes.
3. Stir the Soy-Ginger Sauce to make sure the cornstarch is evenly mixed. Add to the vegetables and bring to a boil. Cook for 3 minutes, until slightly thickened and all vegetables are coated with sauce.
4. Serve with the brown rice.

Look for dried Chinese mushrooms in the Asian section of the store.

Serving size: 13 oz
Servings per recipe: 5
Calories: 317
Total fat: 7 g
Saturated fat: 1 g

!'''! *Soy-Ginger Sauce*

½ c soy sauce
½ c water
 1 tbsp grated ginger
½ c chopped scallions
2 cloves garlic, finely chopped
2 tsp sesame oil
2 tsp chinese vinegar or red wine vinegar
2 tsp sugar
4 c cooked brown rice

1. Mix all ingredients together and let stand for 30 minutes.

Easy! Wonderful! Tart, sweet, salty sauce. Spoon over veggies, salads, pasta, potatoes, and stir-fry.

Serving size: 10 oz
Servings per recipe: 4
Calories: 279
Total fat: 4 g
Saturated fat: 1 g

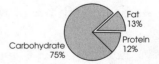

BEANS

¡¡¡¡ *Spicy Red Beans and Rice*

> 1 tbsp vegetable oil
> 2 large onions, diced
> 1 large clove garlic, minced
> 2 large green peppers, diced
> 3 celery stalks, sliced
> 2 bay leaves
> ½ tsp thyme
> ½ tsp cumin
> 1 tsp paprika
> 2 c canned crushed tomatoes
> 1 tbsp cider vinegar
> 1 c vegetable broth, or more if necessary
> 1½ 15-oz cans red kidney beans, rinsed and drained
> ½ tsp hot pepper sauce, or to taste
> 1½ tsp salt, or to taste
> 4 c cooked brown rice

1. Heat oil in a large saucepan. Sauté onion, garlic, green peppers, and celery for 5 minutes. Add all the spices, tomatoes, vinegar, and vegetable broth. Simmer for 10 minutes.
2. Add beans, more vegetable broth if necessary, hot sauce, and salt. Heat through and cook for 5 minutes, until all flavors are blended. Cook rice according to package directions. Remove bay leaves before serving.
3. Serve over white rice.

Cajun, thick, and great.

SERVING SIZE: 16 OZ
Servings per recipe: 6
Calories: 348
Total fat: 4 g
Saturated fat: 0 g

!'!' *Barbecue Baked Beans*

        3 tsp canola oil
        2 cans pinto beans, rinsed and drained
        3 medium onions, 2 chopped, 1 thinly sliced
        2 large green peppers, diced
        4 cloves garlic, minced
        3 tbsp prepared mustard
        2 tbsp chili powder
    1½ tsp salt, or to taste
        1 8-oz can tomato sauce
        ¼ c chili sauce
        ½ c cider vinegar
        ¼ c brown sugar
        ½ tsp hot sauce, or to taste
        2 c vegetable broth

1. Preheat oven to 350°.
2. Heat 2 teaspoons of oil in a skillet. Sauté chopped onion, garlic, and green peppers until onions are lightly browned, about 10 minutes.
3. Add all the other ingredients except sliced onions.
4. Pour mixture into lightly oiled roasting pan using the remaining 1 teaspoon of oil. Arrange sliced onions on

top. Bake for 1 hour, uncovered. The beans should look nice and brown.

Just like Grandma used to make—without the grease. Nothing like baked beans on toast for a quick meal. Baked beans on rice. Baked beans on potatoes. Baked beans everywhere!

SERVING SIZE: 14 OZ
Servings per recipe: 6
Calories: 234
Total fat: 4 g
Saturated fat: 0 g

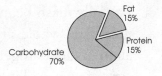

¡!!! *Bean and Corn Burritos*

> *1 c dry red kidney beans or 2 c canned kidney beans*
> *2 c frozen corn, cooked*
> *2 tsp canola oil*
> *1 medium onion, chopped*
> *2 cloves garlic, chopped*
> *½ red pepper, chopped*
> *½ green pepper, chopped*
> *1 jalapeño pepper, seeded and minced*
> *1 tsp basil*
> *½ tsp oregano*
> *2 tbsp cilantro, chopped*
> *1 lb corn tortillas*
> *1 tsp salt, or to taste*
> *1 tsp sugar*

1. Pick over beans, soak them overnight, and discard liquid. Wash and cook, drain, and reserve liquid. If using canned beans, drain and rinse them.
2. Cook corn and blend half into a creamy sauce with a blender, hand blender, or food processor.
3. Heat oil in a pan and sauté onion and garlic for 3 minutes. Add peppers, basil, and oregano, and continue cooking for 5 minutes.
4. Partially mash beans and add to pan. Cook for 2 minutes. Add whole and creamed corn and cilantro. Mix all ingredients together. Add salt and sugar, and check consistency, making sure it is soft and easy to use as a filling. Set aside.
5. Heat tortillas on a hot griddle, 2 or 3 at a time, until they become flexible. Fill them with a few spoonfuls of the filling. Roll up tortilla around the filling.
6. Set aside in a warming pan until all are done. Heat in the oven and serve with salsa. Keep covered to keep tortillas moist.

Mexican heaven!

SERVING SIZE: 12 OZ
Servings per recipe: 4
Calories: 527
Total fat: 6 g
Saturated fat: 1 g

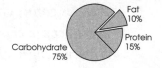

SWEETS

!''! *Apple Fritters*

> 3 medium apples, peeled, cored, and cut into ¼-inch
>   rounds
> 1 c whole wheat flour
> 1 tsp baking powder
> ¼ tsp salt
> ¼ tsp ground cinnamon
> 1 large egg
> 1 c apple juice
> 1 tbsp vegetable oil

1. Dry apples with paper towel and set aside. Apples need to be dry or batter will not stick.
2. Mix flour, baking powder, salt, and cinnamon in a bowl.
3. In a separate bowl, beat egg, juice, and 1¼ teaspoons of vegetable oil. Mix wet and dry ingredients together until there are no lumps.
4. In a nonstick pan, heat ½ teaspoon of oil. Dip apples in batter and let excess drip off. Sauté slices a few at a time. Cook until golden, turn, and brown the other side. Continue until all apples are done. Drain on paper towels.

Top with honey or maple syrup. Easy!

SERVING SIZE: 7 OZ
Servings per recipe: 4
Calories: 254
Total fat: 6 g
Saturated fat: 1 g

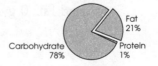

Fat 21%
Carbohydrate 78%
Protein 1%

ᴵ''ᴵ Oatmeal Fruit Cookies

> 2 medium-size ripe bananas (to make 1 c mashed)
> 2 egg whites
> 1 c pitted and chopped dates
> 1½ c rolled oats
> ½ c raisins

1. Preheat oven to 350°.
2. Mash bananas, leaving some chunks. Add egg whites and dates, and mix to make sure dates are separated and well coated.
3. Mix in rolled oats and raisins. Set aside for 10 minutes. Wipe a cookie sheet with a little oil. Place teaspoonful of dough on cookie sheet, and flatten with the back of a spoon.
4. Bake for 20 to 25 minutes, until the edges are lightly browned. Cool and remove from pan. Store well covered in refrigerator or freezer.

Moist, sweet, chewy cookie. Easy, easy, easy—get the kids to help! Double recipe and freeze for later.

SERVING SIZE: 1 OZ
Servings per recipe: 24
Calories: 60
Total fat: trace
Saturated fat: 0 g

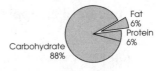

Fat 6%
Protein 6%
Carbohydrate 88%

!!!! *Apple Blueberry Crisp*

1 tsp canola oil

Filling:
4 medium Granny Smith apples, peeled, cored, and
   sliced
1 tbsp lemon juice
1 tsp ground cinnamon
¼ c sugar
1 c frozen blueberries

Topping:
1 c rolled oats
⅓ c unbleached flour
¼ c brown sugar
4 tsp canola oil
½ tsp ground cinnamon
1 tbsp orange juice

1. Preheat oven to 375°.
2. Lightly wipe a 9½-by-11-inch baking dish with 1 teaspoon oil.
3. Mix sliced apples with lemon juice, cinnamon, and
   sugar. Press into baking dish and sprinkle frozen berries on top.
4. Mix topping ingredients and sprinkle over blueberry
   mixture.
5. Bake for 30 minutes, until crumbs look lightly
   browned. Test apples with a fork for tenderness.
6. Enjoy warm or at room temperature.

*Try this one warm with low-fat ice cream melting on top—
then you tell me if you're living in deprivation!*

SERVING SIZE: 4 OZ
Servings per recipe: 9
Calories: 136
Total fat: 3 g
Saturated fat: 0 g

Fat
20%

Carbohydrate
74%

Protein
6%

Epilogue

Dear Boys,

Since I wrote that letter to you, I've had to face the most difficult thing I've ever had to face. I am an alcoholic. The shame and the incredible fear that I felt when I had to face my disease was connected to so many things you'll never understand because you were lucky enough never to be exposed to them, and it was truly the hardest part for me.

My "other" family has so much history, so many circumstances, so much unresolved rage and pain connected to the bottle that it was impossible for me to disconnect from it all and just look at my life and the physical disease of alcoholism that I was born with. When it comes to this disease it never is that clean.

It was impossible for me not to walk through the

shrapnel of so many other wars with alcohol before I could solve my own problem.

My gutter was being at the edge of, being able to see, and sitting in what turned out to be the final ripple of having grown up in a home where this disease stole relationships and destroyed what is right and necessary to grow up whole and healthy. It was standing and looking at this thing spilling over and into our life, your life. That was the end for me.

I could see the next progression of my disease. You growing up in an alcoholic home. My alcoholism becoming your problem . . . that was my gutter because I understand all too well exactly what that means.

That's how I grew up: without the solution, without the healing, without any rhyme or reason for the madness, and it's a horrible way to try and sort out childhood and early adulthood.

So I did what everyone with this disease has to do to change it. First, I took responsibility. Not that I did so willingly. Most of us don't make major changes willingly, you'll find that out soon enough. Change doesn't come easy —have a quick look around to qualify that!

We like convenience, we like habit, we like comfort— even if it's negative, it's still, so much of the time, easier than changing. Change takes courage. To change something, anything, means being willing to look at the truth and feel the loss and shame that so much of the time goes hand in hand with that truth. None of it is comfortable.

And it certainly wasn't for me when I had to look at my truth with alcoholism. But I did. Then I worked really, really hard to get the information I needed to treat what I found out was a physical disease, the disease of alcoholism. In doing that, this book was born. Because the information isn't readily available and it must be (everyone suffering from this disease deserves this information). I had to write about the biochemical treatment that can stop the cravings for alcohol and make sobriety sooooo much easier. I absolutely must stand up and talk about the government, current recovery models, the liquor boys, the AMA, and the deliberate exclusion of the wonderful discoveries and information that can save millions that has been sitting there for the last forty-plus years in the treatment for the disease of alcoholism! How could I keep quiet about something so important?

And in that way, I drag you into my disease. In my standing up and telling my story you will be involved, and in that sense you are still the innocent victims. You are going to have to face the ignorance, the fear, the unwillingness to change, the anger, the incorrect translation of the information that is going to happen the second this book hits the stands and that was my first, and most consuming, thought when I made the decision to write about my alcoholism.

One of the most important lessons sobriety has taught me is truth. The healing power of the absolute truth. The daily, living example that darkness cannot live in light. The beginning of what must be and the end of what should never have been is the opening of the door. The door to:

Discussion
Information
Connection
Application
Movement forward
The truth . . .

Sobriety has given me an opportunity to make you a part of my disease in solution, in healing, and in a positive outcome. My alcoholism has given me the most healing experience of my life. Breaking one of our family's longest, most vicious, and most destructive cycles, in the treatment of, the daily management of, and in healing the damage done by, and finally in understanding what happened in discovering the truth about this disease.

Your love for me and my love for you was, and always will be, one of the most powerful forces in my movement forward. I'm not sure I would have saved myself, but what has been proven to me over and over again in my life is that my love for you requires me to do it, whatever it is, and that's what has saved me every time! In order to be blanketed in the most powerful love of my life, I want to be responsible in, participate in, and continue to grow in that love, and I will continue to work hard to always have that privilege and protection in my life.

I love you,
Mama

Notes

!"!

Introduction

16 *The great majority:* L. Ann Mueller, M.D., and Katherine Ketcham, *Recovering: How to Get and Stay Sober,* 158.

16 *An abnormal metabolism:* James Robert Milam, *Under the Influence,* 16.

16 *This susceptibility exists:* Milam, 15.

16 *Alcoholics have a built-in:* Milam, 16.

16 *Alcoholics don't abuse:* Katherine Ketcham and L. Ann Mueller, M.D., *Eating Right to Live Sober,* 25.

Sober Why

53 *"Alcoholism is tragically":* James Robert Milam, *Under the Influence,* 9.

53 *"an absence of self-discipline":* Milam, 7.

54 *"My opinion is that":* Milam, 6.

54 *"If the federal government":* Milam, 6.

55 *"not happen to believe":* Milam, 7.

60 *"Studies conclude"*: J. Mathews-Larson, *Seven Weeks to Sobriety*, 36.

60 *"When people say"*: *Washington Times*, March 3, 1997.

60 *"Physiology not psychology"*: Milam, 34.

61 *"The alcoholic is generally"*: Milam, 6.

65 *"Alcoholism is known"*: Milam, 6.

65 *"In medical language"*: Milam, 6.

65 *"are ill and victims"*: Mathews-Larson, 38.

66 *"Personality changes are"*: Mathews-Larson, 38.

70 *"Studies conclude"*: Mathews-Larson, 36.

Sober How

127 *"It is no more logical"*: J. Mathews-Larson, *Seven Weeks to Sobriety*, 38.

129 *"Research shows"*: James Robert Milam, *Under the Influence*, 35.

129 *"Abnormal Metabolism—Acetaldehyde"*: Milam, 35.

130 *"This foul-up"*: Katherine Ketcham and L. Ann Mueller, M.D., *Eating Right to Live Sober*, 27.

130 *"The liver mitochondria"*: Milam, 35.

134 *"Like all chronic illnesses"*: Ketcham and Mueller, 25.

136 *"The alcoholic in the early"*: Ketcham and Mueller, 26.

136 *"The early alcoholic"*: Milam, 99.

136 *"During this stage"*: Ketcham and Mueller, 25.

141 *"In addition to"*: Ketcham and Mueller, 54.

141 *"Every drinking alcoholic"*: Ketcham and Mueller, 54.

141 *"Nutritional disease in alcoholics"*: Ketcham and Mueller, 54.

141 *"Every alcoholic has"*: Ketcham and Mueller, 64.

145 *"Alcohol attacks"*: Ketcham and Mueller, 66.

148 *"Sick cells need help"*: Ketcham and Mueller, 76.

149 *"Nutritional therapy will lessen"*: Ketcham and Mueller, 78.

149 *"Such alcoholics typically"*: Ketcham and Mueller, 80.

149 *"Alcohol's massive assault"*: Milam, 73.

152 *"The abstained alcoholic"*: Milam, 78.

155 *"An overwhelming majority"*: Stephen Langer, "Addicted: How to Get Relief Naturally," *Better Nutrition for Today's Living,* May 1990.

155 *"Those receiving nutritional therapy"*: Janet Reid, *Journal of American Dietetic Association,* April 1991.

162 *"The alcoholic reacts physically"*: Ketcham and Mueller, 30.

163 *"The alcoholic's guilt"*: Milam, 68.

177 *"For most of us"*: Jack Trimpey, *The Small Book,* 50.

186 *"The beginning of quitting"*: Trimpey, 51.

187 *"The biochemical makeup"*: interview with J. Mathews-Larson.

190 *EFAs have been shown:* R. C. Reitz, "Dietary Fatty Acids and Alcohol: Effects on Cellular Membranes," *Alcohol Alcohol* 28 (1): 59–71, 59.

191 *In fact,* Rhodiola rosea: A. S. Saratikov and E. A. Kraznov, "*Rhodiola rosea* Is a valuable Medicinal Plant," *Tomsk University Publisher* 1987: 252; D. M. Mayerski, "The Use of *Rhodiola rosea* Extract in Liver Detoxification," *Applied Medicine and Pharmacology* 1967: 12–19.

205 *"has been implicated"*: Elson M. Haas, M.D., *Staying Healthy with Nutrition,* 33.

206 *"Low blood sugar"*: Milam, 154.

206 *"Recovering alcoholics often"*: Judy Myers, "Sugar Addicting Seesaw," *Alcohol and Addiction Magazine,* June 1988.

206 *"The symptoms do not simply"*: Milam, 75.

207 *"Before and after"*: *Journal of American Dietetic Association,* April 1991.

211 *"you cause a craving"*: Milam, 154.

214 *"During temporary shortages"*: Ketcham and Mueller, 97.

215 *"Hypoglycemia is not"*: *Mayo Clinic Family Health Book,* 710.

215 *"Many people claim"*: *The Wellness Encyclopedia,* 131.

218 *"In 1981 a survey"*: Ketcham and Mueller, 90.

219 *"Recovering alcoholics often"*: Judy Myers, *Alcoholism and Addiction Magazine,* June 1988.

219 *"From an ice cream cone"*: *Alcoholism and Addiction Magazine.* (From a Lexis/Nexis search by the author).

252 *"In our mind's ear"*: Trimpey, 57.

261 *"We think in pictures"*: Trimpey, 57.

Reading
Resources

!!!!

Alcohol and Recovery

Larson, J. Mathews, Ph.D. *Seven Weeks to Sobriety.* New York: Ballantine Books, 1992.

Milam, Dr. James R. and Katherine Ketcham. *Under the Influence.* New York: Bantam Books, 1981.

Mueller, L. Ann, M.D., and Katherine Ketcham. *Recovering: How to Get and Stay Sober.* New York: Bantam Books, 1987.

Williams, Roger J. *Alcoholism: The Nutritional Approach.* Austin, Tex.: University of Texas Press, 1959.

Ketcham, Katherine and L. Ann Mueller, M.D. *Eating Right to Live Sober.* New York: Penguin Books, 1983.

Goodwin, Donald, M.D. *Is Alcoholism Hereditary?* New York: Oxford University Press, 1976.

Trimpey, Jack. *The Small Book.* New York: Bantam Doubleday Dell, 1989.

Nutrition

Davis, Adelle. *Let's Get Well.* New York: New American Library, 1984.

Nutrition Almanac. New York: McGraw-Hill, 1990.

Null, Gary. *The Complete Guide to Health and Nutrition.* New York: Doubleday, 1983.

Goldbeck, Nikki and David Goldbeck. *The Supermarket Handbook.* New York: New American Library, 1984.

Haas, Elson M., M.D. *Staying Healthy with Nutrition.* Berkeley, Calif.: Celestial Arts, 1992.

McDougall, John A., M.D., and Mary A. McDougall. *The McDougall Plan.* Clinton, N.J.: New Win Publishing, 1985.

Kilham, Christopher S. *The Bread and Circus Whole Food Bible.* New York: Addison-Wesley, 1991.

Hypoglycemia / Low Blood Sugar

Dufty, William. *Sugar Blues.* New York: Warner Books, 1993.

Saunders, Jeraldine and Dr. Harvey M. Ross. *Hypoglycemia: The Disease Your Doctor Won't Treat.* New York: Pinnacle Books, 1981.

Abrahamson, E. M., M.D., and A. W. Pezet. *Body, Mind and Sugar.* New York: Henry Holt & Co., 1951.

Krimmel, Edward and Patricia Krimmel. *The Low Blood Sugar Handbook.* Franklin, 1991.

Airola, Paavo, Ph.D. *Hypoglycemia: A Better Approach.* Health Plus Pub., 1977.

Brennan, Dr. R. O. and William C. Mulligan. *Nutrigenetics: New Concepts for Relieving Hypoglycemia.* New York: New American Library, 1977.

Appleton, Nancy, Ph.D. *Lick The Sugar Habit.* Wayne, N.J.: Avery Publishing Group, 1996.

Nutritional Cookbooks

Beasley, Dr. Joseph, M.D. *Food for Recovery: The Complete Nutritional Companion for Recovering from Alcoholism,* New York: Crown, 1994.

Krimmel, Patricia and Edward Krimmel. *The Low Blood Sugar Cookbook.* Franklin, 1986.

Davis, Francyne. *The Low Blood Sugar Cookbook.* New York: Bantam Books, 1985.

Buchman Ewald, Ellen. *Recipes for a Small Planet.* New York: Ballantine Books, 1983.

Ford J. *Deaf Smith Country Cookbook.* Wayne, N.J.: Avery Publishing Group, 1992.

Powter, Susan. *Food.* New York: Simon & Schuster, 1995.

Katzen, Mollie. *The Moosewood Cookbook.* Berkeley, Calif.: Ten Speed Press, 1992.

Davis, Adelle. *Let's Cook It Right.* New York: Harcourt Brace, 1962.

Treatment Centers

!!!

St. Helena Hospital and
Health Center—John
McDougall
650 Sanitarium Road
Deerpark CA 94576
1-800-454-4673
1-800-358-9195

Health Recovery Center—
J. Mathews Larson
3255 Hennepin Avenue,
South
Minneapolis, MN 55408
1-800-554-9155
(612) 827-7800